W0081388

Advance Praise for
Poems by Presidents: The First-Ever Anthology

From Madison's collegiate satires to Harding's racy romantic rhymes, this anthology has something to surprise and delight even the most dedicated history buff. It will teach you something about our presidents' personal lives, their poetic talents, and even their political ambitions.

—Craig Fehrman, author of *Author in Chief:*
The Untold Story of Our Presidents and the Books They Wrote

Well-written, thoroughly researched, and impeccably organized, *Poems by Presidents* explores an intriguing and unexpected side to many American presidents: they wrote poetry! In this excellent anthology of presidential poems, Michael Croland offers us a new way to celebrate some of our most celebrated leaders.

—Susan Katz, author of *The President's Stuck in the Bathtub*

This distinctive collection is a pleasure to read and enjoy. It provides another dimension to our awareness of the personalities and talents of many of our presidents. Who knew that Warren G. Harding wrote erotically explicit love poems? And that many of our presidents turned to poetry for emotional and literary sustenance? Appropriately, the president-poet most fully represented in this excellent anthology is the most talented poet among our presidents, John Quincy Adams, followed by Abraham Lincoln, who was a minor poet in poetry and a major poet in prose.

—Fred Kaplan, author of *His Masterly Pen:*
A Biography of Jefferson the Writer

Michael Croland has assembled an interesting and unexpected anthology of presidential poetry. Witness George Washington's teenage heartache, or blush at Warren Harding's rhyming adultery. *Poems by Presidents* leaves the reader with a better understanding of the concealed humanity often buried within the seemingly stoic men who have held our nation's highest office.

—Michael B. Costanzo, author of *Author in Chief: The Presidents as Writers from Washington to Trump*

Chief executive, commander-in-chief, head of state—and poet? Yes, indeed! This unique collection by US presidents, featuring poems ranging from spiritual to humorous to erotic, is surprising, fascinating, and humanizing. There is always something new to learn about these gentlemen—and this book proves it.

—Marilyn Singer, author of *Rutherford B., Who Was He?: Poems about Our Presidents* and *Have You Heard about Lady Bird?: Poems about Our First Ladies*

A wonderful volume, full of keen insights into a wide array of American presidents. . . . The superb focus of this book brings fascinating details to light.

—Jonathan Gross, editor of *Thomas Jefferson's Scrapbooks*

Author Michael Croland has captured the essence of a unique piece of Americana: the poetic verse of America's presidents. Readers can gain a unique insight into the inner thoughts and feelings of our leaders, providing those who are interested or curious some additional understanding of their personalities.

—Jeffrey A. Margolis, author of *The President's Pen*

Poems by Presidents

★ ★ ★ ★ ★ ★ ★ ★ ★ ★ ★ ★ ★

THE FIRST-EVER ANTHOLOGY

Poems by Presidents

★ ★ ★ ★ ★ ★ ★ ★ ★ ★ ★ ★ ★

THE FIRST-EVER ANTHOLOGY

EDITED BY MICHAEL CROLAND

DOVER PUBLICATIONS, GARDEN CITY, NEW YORK

Copyright © 2023 by Dover Publications
All rights reserved.

Poems by Presidents: The First-Ever Anthology is a new work, first published by Dover Publications in 2023.

Library of Congress Cataloging-in-Publication Data

Names: Croland, Michael, editor.
Title: Poems by presidents : the first-ever anthology / edited by Michael Croland.
Description: Garden City : Dover Publications, 2023. | Includes bibliographical
references. | Summary: "This first-ever anthology features poems by eleven presidents
who, through good times and bad, turned to poetry to express themselves. This
compelling collection brings presidents' literary pursuits to light, unveiling their deepest
thoughts and emotions. Highlights include George Washington's teenage romantic
yearnings, Thomas Jefferson's death-bed adieu, John Quincy Adams's sonnet
memorializing his father, Abraham Lincoln's mockery of the Confederacy, Woodrow
Wilson's humorous limericks, Warren G. Harding's steamy love poems to his mistress,
and Ronald Wilson Reagan's existential reflections. Appendixes explore additional
presidents who wrote poetry, misattributions, prose formatted as verse, and fondness
for poetry. Poems by Presidents is a rewarding resource for poetry lovers and readers
interested in presidential biographies and American history."—Provided by publisher.
Identifiers: LCCN 2023011516 | ISBN 9780486851532 (trade paperback)
Subjects: LCSH: American poetry. | Presidents' writings, American. | BISAC: POETRY
/ Subjects & Themes / Political & Protest | HISTORY / United States / General |
LCGFT: Poetry.
Classification: LCC PS591.P67 P64 2023 | DDC 811—dc23/eng/20230712
LC record available at https://lccn.loc.gov/2023011516

Manufactured in the United States of America
85153201
www.doverpublications.com

To Tamara and Robin

Contents

Acknowledgments

Thank you to Peter Lenz and Susan Rattiner for your support of this anthology. Thank you to the rest of the Dover team, especially Peter Donahue, Andrew Sliwoski, and Marie Zaczkiewicz.

Thank you to Susan Rattiner and Ilene Rattiner for your assistance deciphering handwritten poems.

Thank you, John Grafton, for your guidance.

Thank you to the Massachusetts Historical Society—particularly Hannah Elder, Neal Millikan, and Sara Martin—for providing John Quincy Adams's "A Theory of Comets: To the Comet Seen at Quincy, 6. October 1825: A Sonnet" and "On Witnessing the Ascension in a Balloon of Madame Johnson, a Widowed Mother, at Castle Garden, New York, 20. October 1825: A Sonnet" from the Adams Family Papers.

John Tyler's "Oh child of my love thou wert born for a day" and all the selections by Warren G. Harding came from the Library of Congress. Thank you to Peter Armenti from the Researcher and Reference Services Division; Julie Miller, Edith A. Sandler, and Lara Szypszak from the Manuscript Division; and Morgan Davis from the Music Division.

Thank you to Earl Gregg Swem Library at William & Mary Libraries, particularly Carolyn Wilson and Kaitlyn Weathers, for providing Tyler's "Virginia" and "To M. G. B." from the Tyler Family Papers.

Woodrow Wilson's "A River's Course," "A Song," "To E. L. A. on Her Birthday," and "On Board Steamship Anchoria" originally appeared in *The Papers of Woodrow Wilson*, published by Princeton University Press.

Permission to publish Ronald Wilson Reagan's "Life" and "Time" was granted by the Ronald Reagan Presidential Foundation and Institute.

Thank you to the Franklin D. Roosevelt Presidential Library, particularly Virginia Lewick, for providing the verse recited by Roosevelt.

Thank you to Yale University Library's Beinecke Rare Book and Manuscript Library, Woodrow Wilson Presidential Library, George H. W. Bush Presidential Library & Museum, Barack Obama Presidential Library, National Library of Australia, and the New York Public Library's Scan & Deliver and General Research Division.

Thank you, Tamara, for your love and patience.

Poetically speaking, here's a shout-out to Robin, Mom, Jack, Nancy, Benjamin, Alan, Marla, Dan, Lisa, Zachary, and Zoey.

Introduction

"There is more of a nation's politics to be gotten out of its poetry than out of all its systematic writers upon public affairs and constitutions."

—Woodrow Wilson

Even Woodrow Wilson, one of the most talented presidential poets, would have been surprised to find his verse collected and published. An anthology for general readers was not his intended purpose or audience. But presidents' poetry reveals their minds and spirits. It provides insight into their biographies and, by extension, American history.

Thomas Jefferson composed a "death-bed adieu." John Quincy Adams memorialized his father with a sonnet. John Tyler mourned his infant daughter with a moving elegy. Abraham Lincoln lampooned Robert E. Lee and the Confederacy. Several presidents used poetry to convey their romantic yearnings. Through good times and bad, and through triumph and struggle, presidents turned to poetry to express themselves. Their verse is interwoven with the fabric of their lives.

A love of language, especially precise wording, connects poetry to the prowess of a gifted scribe or orator. The selections in this anthology show that poetry can correlate with writing ability, public speaking skills, and intelligence. These attributes are essential components of a president's job and metrics by which their legacies are measured.

Americans revere the select few who have served as our nation's chief executive. They are the namesakes of our schools, roads, and airports. Their personal stories, and their successes and failures, form the core of what is taught in American history classes and account for countless popular books and movies. *Poems by Presidents: The First-Ever Anthology* offers a unique look behind the curtain of what made these presidents tick.

Scope

The canon of presidential poets consists of the fifteen presidents in this book's chapters and Appendix A. This anthology features poems by eleven presidents, with the chapters arranged by the sequence of their presidencies: George Washington, Thomas Jefferson, James Madison, John Quincy Adams, John Tyler, Abraham Lincoln, Ulysses S. Grant, James Abram Garfield, Woodrow Wilson, Warren G. Harding, and Ronald Wilson Reagan. Appendix A considers poetry by four presidents whose verse is not included: Jimmy Carter, George Bush, Barack Obama, and Joseph R. Biden. Appendixes B, C, and D explore misattributions, prose formatted as verse, and fondness for poetry, respectively. The four appendixes address an additional nineteen presidents not featured in the chapters.

The fifteen presidential poets include individuals who only wrote one poem—Jefferson and Grant—as well as the most prolific, Adams, who wrote about 350 surviving poems. Adams was one of two presidents who published a poetry book in his lifetime; the other was Carter. Adams was one of two presidents whose verse was collected and published posthumously; the other was Lincoln, although the books of his poetry are rather slender.

Adams was one of two presidents who hit the trifecta of writing poetry before, during, and after his presidency; the other was Tyler. Lincoln and Biden penned verse before and during their time in office, and Wilson and Carter did so before and after their presidencies. Seven presidents only tried their hand at poetry earlier in life. Bush was unique for only writing poetry as a sitting president. Jefferson was the lone president whose poetic output came exclusively after he had left the White House.

Poems by presidents cross party lines and ideological stances. They span many topics and styles. They take varied forms, including acrostic, ballad, elegy, epic, free verse, genethliacum, haiku, limerick, list poem, ode, and sonnet. Besides being political, they can be erotic, existential, humorous, religious, or romantic. Some poems in this volume are well-known, and some may never have appeared in print previously.

The first presidential poetry was written by Washington in 1749–50, and the tradition continues to the present day. Between the main text and the appendixes, this anthology touches on two-thirds of the presidents, including the nineteen most recent ones.

Origins and Context

The present volume grew out of my last two anthologies, *There Once Was a Limerick Anthology* and *Acrostic Poetry: The First-Ever Anthology*, which were published by Dover Publications in 2022 and 2023, respectively. The former includes a limerick by Wilson, and the latter features acrostics by Washington, Adams, and Grant. The realization that several presidents had written poetry inspired a quest to find more.

Poems by Presidents is the first anthology of presidents' poems, but the idea is not new. In a biography of Washington published in 1926, Rupert Hughes looked at the first president's poems as well as verse from Lincoln and Wilson. Hughes noted, "An interesting anthology of the poetry of our Presidents might be made."

Two sources did commendable work on the subject. Peter Armenti, the English and American literature specialist for the Main Reading Room at the Library of Congress (LC), created the LC's "Presidents as Poets: Poetry Written by United States Presidents." This impressive microsite features ten presidents who wrote poetry and draws on the LC's vast holdings. While the content is not as wide-ranging as a book, it was an invaluable starting point for research.

Paul J. Ferlazzo published *Poetry and the American Presidency* in 2012. He explored the relationship between presidents and poetry, focusing more on presidents' fondness for verse than their original compositions. For example, Ferlazzo devoted a chapter to Jefferson but did not mention that he wrote at least one poem. Ferlazzo did, however, feature poems by other presidents. He included chapters about Theodore Roosevelt and John Fitzgerald Kennedy, who did not write any poems; both are relegated to the last appendix in the present volume. Presidents' appreciation for poetry, for which *Poetry and the American Presidency* is the best resource, is a key part of the context presented in this anthology's chapter introductions.

The other larger context that presidential poetry is a part of is presidential writing. This macrocosm likewise figures prominently in chapter introductions. In 2020, Craig Fehrman published two exceptional books about presidents' literary offerings, *Author in Chief: The Untold Story of Our Presidents and the Books They Wrote* and *The Best Presidential Writing: From 1789 to the Present.* Jeffrey A. Margolis's *The President's Pen: Reflections on Presidential Literature* (2020) and Michael B. Costanzo's *Author in Chief: The Presidents as Writers from Washington to Trump* (2019) deserve honorable mention. I am grateful that these recent books provided me with a crash course in presidential writing.

In selecting the contents for the present volume, I began with the presidents discussed on "Presidents as Poets" and in *Poetry and the American Presidency.* Then I cast a wider net and found additional poems not included in either of those sources by Adams, Tyler, Garfield, Wilson, Harding, Carter, and Reagan. I added Bush and Biden to the canon of presidential poets.

Varied Quality

Adams is the indisputable star of presidential poetry. He penned more than seven times as many extant poems as any other president. Writing poetry was a key part of his life, not a rarity. Some of his oeuvre, especially "The Wants of Man," is magnificent, and several of his poems have been featured in multiple anthologies. It was a challenge to limit how much of his verse appears in the present volume.

Not every presidential poet is in the same league as Adams. In *Author in Chief,* Fehrman thought footnotes were the best venue to acknowledge the poetry of Washington, Madison, and

Harding. Regarding Madison's verse, Fehrman quipped, "Out of respect for the presidency, it will be confined to a footnote." In *Poems by Presidents*, Madison's poems graduate from a footnote to a full chapter.

While this volume contains some stellar poems, others do not pass muster. They still made the cut. They still shine a light on the inner workings of pivotal figures who held the highest office in the land. In the chapter introductions, this anthology largely shies away from pointing out inferior quality. It's beside the point. A brief overview is nevertheless in order.

The label "doggerel" has been thrown around with some presidential poets. The National Archives' Founders Online site classified Madison's three poems as doggerel. Lincoln applied the term to his three longer poems, which are among the standouts in this volume.

In *A Poet's Glossary*, Edward Hirsch explained that doggerel is a long-standing "derogatory term for bad poetry." He classified it as "a trivial form of verse, loosely constructed and rhythmically irregular," that "often has forced rhymes, faulty meters, and trite sentiments." He quoted George Saintsbury's distinction between doggerel that fails to meet the poet's intended quality standards and doggerel that revels in "a willful licentiousness which is excused by the felicitous result." The label "doggerel" has varied meanings, and it is not constructive to parse which is applicable to specific examples. The term will not be used going forward.

Readers may form their own opinions about the poetic merits of the material. The poor quality of some selections does not detract from their biographical and historical significance.

Editor's Note

Each chapter begins with the president's name, followed by his birth and death years. The ordinal number and years of his presidency appear next.

Titles of poems are included where applicable. Some selections are untitled.

All the poems in this volume were definitively written by the presidents identified unless otherwise indicated. Additional poems attributed to Jefferson and Lincoln are not included because their authorship is dubious.

Some poems have appeared in different versions. For example, some were edited in between their original writing and their publication. The versions in the present volume are the result of editorial discretion. Scholars are encouraged to dig deeper in order to choose between inconsistencies.

Readers should be forewarned that Harding's salacious verse is explicit.

Bonus Material

The bonus material webpage for *Poems by Presidents* offers additional content of interest to readers. Visit the webpage at www.doverpublications.com/0486851532.

The webpage features Adams's "O God, with Goodness All Thy Own" plus links to the complete text of both of his poetry books, *Poems of Religion and Society* and *Dermot Mac Morrogh, or The Conquest of Ireland*.

The musical score of Tyler's "Virginia," arranged by his daughter Letitia Tyler Semple, is included.

Readers can listen to Carter recite "Rachel" and "The Pasture Gate" and watch him read "Considering the Void." Links are provided for five additional poems by Carter: "Rosalynn," "Some Things I Love," "A Reflection of Beauty in Washington," "Progress Does Not Always Come Easy," and "Itinerant Songsters Visit Our Village."

Links are provided for Lincoln's "To Rosa Haggard," Reagan's "State Budget," and Obama's "Pop" and "Underground."

All of the content linked to on the webpage was accessible as of this writing. Dover Publications and the editor of this anthology are not responsible if any of the materials are no longer available online.

Michael Croland
March 2023

George Washington

1732–99

≈❧≈

1ˢᵗ president (1789–97)

As a general, George Washington led the Continental Army to victory in the Revolutionary War. As the beloved first president, he set precedents that steered the US in the right direction, including staying neutral in foreign wars, presenting the State of the Union as a speech to Congress, and only serving two terms.

Washington's letters, diaries, and other written documents number in the thousands, but he left behind only two poems. Both appear as pages inserted into his diary from when he worked as a surveyor in Virginia. They are dated 1749–50.

Both poems express a teenager's infatuation with young women in his life. Both mention a dart from Cupid. The first selection is an acrostic for his crush, Frances Alexander. A proper acrostic would have spelled out her name with the initial letter of each line, but Washington abandoned the effort before composing the final four lines. The identity of the person whom the second poem addresses is unknown. The poems are widely attributed to Washington, but some scholars speculate that he might have copied them from another source.

From your bright sparkling Eyes, I was undone;
Rays, you have more transparent than the sun,
Amidst its glory in the rising Day,
None can you equal in your bright array;
Constant in your calm and unspotted Mind;
Equal to all, but will to none Prove kind,
So knowing, seldom one so Young, you'l Find
Ah! woe's me, that I should Love and conceal,
Long have I wish'd, but never dare reveal,
Even though severly Loves Pains I feel;
Xerxes that great, was't free from Cupids Dart,
And all the greatest Heroes, felt the smart.

Oh Ye Gods why should my Poor Resistless Heart
Stand to oppose thy might and Power
At Last surrender to cupids feather'd Dart
And now lays Bleeding every Hour
For her that's Pityless of my grief and Woes
And will not on me Pity take
Ile sleep amongst my most Inveterate Foes
And with gladness never with to Wake
In deluding sleepings let my Eyelids close
That in an enraptured Dream I may
In a soft lulling sleep and gentle repose
Possess those joys denied by Day

Thomas Jefferson

1743–1826

∽

3rd president (1801–09)

Thomas Jefferson was one of the most significant Founding Fathers. As president, he doubled the young nation's size through the Louisiana Purchase and improved its economic standing.

Jefferson was a celebrated writer, remembered for standout works like the Declaration of Independence and *Notes on the State of Virginia*. In *His Masterly Pen: A Biography of Jefferson the Writer*, Fred Kaplan praised Jefferson's prose for being "of the highest literary and intellectual quality," noting that his "brilliance as a writer is a key to his personality and public service."

From circa 1758 to 1772, Jefferson maintained a commonplace book with newspaper clippings consisting mostly of poems but also prose. In *Poetry and the American Presidency*, Paul J. Ferlazzo explained that Jefferson "gleaned from" poetry "the philosophical ideas and the moral rules of life" as well as "the practical aspects of . . . how to write or speak well." Ferlazzo added, "He valued the use of effective imagery, the artistic turn of phrase, and the use of the best words for one's speech or writing."

From 1801 to 1809, coinciding with his presidency, Jefferson kept two scrapbooks devoted to nearly 900 poems he found in newspapers. In *Thomas Jefferson's Scrapbooks*, an edited volume featuring highlights from these scrapbooks, Jonathan Gross observed, "To read the poetry Jefferson admired . . . is to become indoctrinated in the values of the early Republic." Jefferson also helped his granddaughters create poetry scrapbooks of their own.

Despite Jefferson's long-standing appreciation of poetry, he definitively only wrote one poem—in the waning days of his life. The bedridden Jefferson composed "A Death-Bed Adieu from Th. J. to

M. R." for his daughter Martha Randolph. Two days before he passed away in 1826, he told her where she could find the farewell poem. Some scholars have attributed an unfinished poem—"To Ellen," intended for his granddaughter—to Jefferson, but he likely did not write it.

A Death-Bed Adieu from Th. J. to M. R.

Life's visions are vanished, its dreams are no more;
Dear friends of my bosom, why bathed in tears?
I go to my fathers, I welcome the shore
Which crowns all my hopes or which buries my cares.
Then farewell, my dear, my lov'd daughter, adieu!
The last pang of life is in parting from you!
Two seraphs await me long shrouded in death;
I will bear them your love on my last parting breath.

James Madison
1751–1836

~~~

4th president (1809–17)

During his presidency, James Madison oversaw the War of 1812, the Second Bank of the United States, and the first protective tariff. He was the Father of the Constitution, devising the framework for the document's guiding principles.

A key part of his promotion of the Constitution was the Federalist Papers. Madison, Alexander Hamilton, and John Jay wrote this series of eighty-five articles, which explained the ideas behind the Constitution and encouraged New York to support ratification. Madison penned twenty-nine of the essays, including the most influential one, in which he argued against the notion that democracy was only feasible for small states.

As significant as his writing was, Madison did not pride himself as a poet. He had never "been favored with the Inspiration of the Muses," he told John Quincy Adams in 1822. Madison wrote his only verse in 1771–72, when he was an undergraduate at the College of New Jersey, which is now Princeton University. He was a member of the American Whig Society, which had a rivalry with another student organization, the Cliosophian Society. In the final battle of a "paper war"—in which the groups attacked each other with heated writing, typically in verse—Madison wrote three of the Whigs' nineteen pieces. "A Poem against the Tories," which calls out several Cliosophians by name, features Madison's sole poetic innovation: ending with a semicolon. The editor of a book of poetry by another Whig contributor dubbed Madison's selections "the worst of the lot," adding, "No patriotic citizen will ever venture to resurrect them."

The Aerial Journey of the Poet Laureat of the Cliosophic Society

The rising sun his beams had shed
And each affrighted star had fled
When tuneful Spring in rural lays
Began to mourn his doleful case
New-englands sons around him came
And many a wanton ruddy dame
Who view'd him nigh a purling stream
Rais'd on a stump to sing his dream.
That very dream in which they say
His soul broke loose from mortal clay
And sought the muses dome on high
Resolv'd with all his art to try
To steal a spark of wit from thence
A scourge for whiggish impudence.
But hear the very words he spoke
As from his quivering lips they broke
"Hail gentle shepherds of the grove
Your flocks about this mead may rove
While you attend my mournful tale
And echo sounds it thro' the vale
Soon as the lamp of day was gone
And evening shades oerspread the lawn
Tir'd with the business of the day
Down on the tender grass I lay.
When sleep had clos'd my slumbering eyes
I spurn'd the earth & pierc'd the skies
Thro' unknown tracts of air I flew
And pas'd by worlds of various hue
Beseeching every thing to tell
The place on which the Muses dwell.

At length, when coasting thro' the spheres
Apollo's song invades my ears
With all the sweet harmonious nine
Whose warbling notes in concert join.
Then by degrees their domes I spy'd
Which blaz'd around on every side
Straight to apollo's hall I went
Half dead with fear, my breath quite spent
Hoping somehow to lurk beneath
And rob him of a laurel wreath
And then a poet laureat rise
The dread of whigs of every size
But while I walk'd about the hall
apollo with the muses all
Came rushing in upon the thief
I cry'd in vain for some relief
The god of day provok'd to find
A villain of so base a mind
Seiz'd on a cudgel rough & great
& mash'd my jaws & crazy pate
Euterpe then a dishclout brought
With grease & boiling water fraught
And well beswitched my sides & back
Which lost its hide at every whack
Urania threw a chamber pot
Which from beneath her bed she brought
And struck my eyes & ears & nose
Repeating it with lusty blows.
In such a pickle then I stood
Trickling on every side with blood
When Clio, ever grateful muse
Sprinkled my head with healing dews

Then took me to her private room
And straight an Eunuch out I come
My voice to render more melodious
A recompence for sufferings odious
She brought me to the earth again
And quel'd the Tumults of my brain
Softly whispering in my ear
While she dropt the parting tear
Dear friend accept this last behest
Conceal thy folly in thy breast
Forbear to write & only sing
And future sons shall talk of Spring
But mark me well if e'er you try
In poetry with Whigs to vie
Your nature's bounds you then will pass
And be transformed into an ass
Then brother shepherds pity Spring
Who dares not write but only sing—
—When thus he finished his complaint
He quit the stump & off he went
But soon forgot what Clio said
And wrote an ode & then essay'd
to sing an hymn & lo! he bray'd
And now he stands an ass confessed
Of every scribbling fool, the Jest

Clio's Proclamation

Whereas a certain mongrel race
of tawney hide & grizly face
Have dar'd to prostitute my name
To raise the scribbling fools to fame
I hereby send this Proclamation
To every land & every nation
Declaring it my full intention
To free the world from this convention
And as a sanction to my word
I'll drive the dogs with fire & sword
Hedlong down to Pluto's coast
There in boiling flames to roast
And then their bodies I'll resign
To gnawing worms & hungry swine
Or to manure the farmers field
For much of dung their trunks will yield
Very like it in their nature
As sprung from every filthy creature
But first selecting from McOrkle
And every other stinking mortal
Whate'er may be of use to those
From whom the wicked wretches rose
The poet Laureat head who scoops
May make a drum for yankey troops
B'ing quite as empty & as sounding
His skull full thick to bear the pounding
While eckley's skin & jakes together
When tan'd will make a side of leather
Just fit to cloath McOrkle bum
Which now becomes a battering ram

And plac'd before a city wall
Will ward off many a whizzing ball
And by its monstrous stench may save
Ten thousand yankes from the grave.
Great Allen founder of the crew
If right I guess must keep a stew
The lecherous rascal there will find
A place just suited to his mind
May whore & pimp & drink & swear
Nor more the garb of christians wear
And free Nassau from such a pest
A dunce a fool an ass at best.

A Poem against the Tories

Of late our muse keen satire drew
And humourous thoughts in vollies flew
Because we took our foes for men
Who might deserve a decent pen
A gross mistake with brutes we fight
And goblins from the realms of night
With lice collected from the beds
Where Spring & Craig lay down their heads
Sometimes a goat steps on the pump
Which animates old Warford's trunk
Sometimes a poisonous toad appears
Which Eckley's yellow carcuss bears
And then to grace us with a bull
Forsooth they show McOrkles skull
And that the Ass may not escape
He takes the poet Laureat's shape
The screetch owl too comes in the train
Which leap'd from Alexander's brain
Just as he scratch'd his grisly head
Which people say is made of lead.
Come noble whigs, disdain these sons
Of screech owls, monkeys, & baboons
Keep up your minds to humourous themes
And verdant meads & flowing streams
Untill this tribe of dunces find
The baseness of their grovelling mind
And skulk within their dens together
Where each ones stench will kill his brother;

John Quincy Adams
1767–1848

❧

6th president (1825–29)

In the administrations of four of the first five presidents, John Quincy Adams served as a minister to various foreign countries or the secretary of state. As the sixth president, he improved the country's infrastructure with roads and canals. After being a senator earlier in his career, he served in the House of Representatives for the last seventeen years of his life. He devoted more than a half century to public service. But if Adams had his druthers, he would have made his name as a writer and poet.

"Could I have chosen my own genius and condition, I would have made myself a great poet," wrote Adams. Separately, he explained, "Literature has been the charm of my life, and could I have carved out my own fortunes, to literature would my whole life have been devoted. I have been a lawyer for bread, and a Statesman at the call of my Country."

Adams dreamed of composing a work that would boost the reputation of American literature internationally. While significant literary fame eluded him, his accomplishments are laudable. His fifty-one-volume diary, which he started when he was twelve years old, impressively documents the life of a singular figure. His history of weights and measurements, report on manufacturing, and Supreme Court argument in the *Amistad* case are prose masterpieces.

In terms of quality and quantity, Adams was a poet to a far greater extent than any other president. He wrote verse from ages fifteen to eighty-one, leaving behind approximately 350 extant poems. By and large, he considered them good but not up to the standards of the poets he admired or capable of improving the nation's literary standing. On paper and in his head, Adams composed poems whenever he could make time, including during church sermons and while out for a walk. He wrote poems to take his mind off his political responsibilities, often amusing himself as well as friends and family. In *John Quincy Adams: American Visionary*, Fred Kaplan called Adams "an excellent versifier and rhymer, with an abundance of learned skill and a touch of estimable talent," whose "poems are often graceful, witty, immediate, and engaging."

Adams wrote an epic poem, *Dermot Mac Morrogh, or The Conquest of Ireland*, in 1831. As he explained in the preface, he hoped that recounting England's conquest of Ireland in the twelfth century through "the garb of poetry" would make the historical tale fascinating to readers. His depiction of King Henry II was a commentary on the scandal-ridden presidency of Adams's successor, Andrew Jackson.

In 1848, the year that Adams passed away, two of his congressional colleagues published *Poems of Religion and Society*, a collection of his shorter poems. The publisher's note boasted, "Many of his minor pieces have wit, humor, grace, and tenderness, and they are all informed with wisdom and various learning."

Numerous poems in the book are religious, and they are among Adams's strongest. The publisher's note declared that Adams's hymns were "among the finest devotional lyrics in our language." His utmost satisfaction came from hearing "For Thee in Zion Waiteth Praise"—his adaptation of King David's Psalm 65—set to music in his church:

> [N]o words can express the sensations with which I heard it sung. Were it possible to compress into one pulsation of the heart the pleasure which, in the whole period of my life, I have enjoyed in praise from the lips of mortal man, it would not weigh a straw to balance the ecstasy of delight which streamed from my eyes as the organ pealed and the choir of voices sung the praise of the Almighty God from the soul of David, adapted to my native tongue by me.

The standout in *Poems of Religion and Society* is "The Wants of Man." Originally published in 1841, it was Adams's most popular secular poem during his lifetime. He wrote it as a distraction from stressful debate over a revenue bill in the House. Although the desires expressed are mostly secular, the focus ultimately turns religious. "The Wants of Man" received renewed attention when Ralph Waldo Emerson included an abridged version in *Parnassus*, an anthology of his favorite poems, in 1874.

The only poems in this chapter that did not appear in *Poems of Religion and Society* are the last three selections. These sonnets are likely the only poems in this chapter that Adams wrote while he was president. Upon reading his thoughts about comets and a hot-air balloon passenger, both from 1825, it is hard to imagine recent presidents expressing comparable sentiments, in either verse or prose. Adams composed the final sonnet in memory of his father—the second president, John Adams—on his birthday in 1826, several months after he passed away. The poem commends the elder Adams's legacy of championing freedom and criticizing slavery. The younger Adams wrote the sonnet entirely in a shorthand made up of symbols.

The Wants of Man

"Man wants but little here below,
Nor wants that little long." —*Goldsmith's Hermit*

I.

"Man wants but little here below,
 Nor wants that little long."
'Tis not with me exactly so,
 But 'tis so in the song.
My wants are many, and if told
 Would muster many a score;
And were each wish a mint of gold,
 I still should long for more.

II.

What first I want is daily bread,
 And canvas backs and wine;
And all the realms of nature spread
 Before me when I dine.
Four courses scarcely can provide
 My appetite to quell,
With four choice cooks from France, beside,
 To dress my dinner well.

III.

What next I want, at heavy cost,
 Is elegant attire;—
Black sable furs, for winter's frost,
 And silks for summer's fire,
And Cashmere shawls, and Brussels lace
 My bosom's front to deck,
And diamond rings my hands to grace,
 And rubies for my neck.

IV.

And then I want a mansion fair,
A dwelling house, in style,
Four stories high, for wholesome air—
A massive marble pile;
With halls for banquets and balls,
All furnished rich and fine;
With stabled studs in fifty stalls,
And cellars for my wine.

V.

I want a garden and a park,
My dwelling to surround—
A thousand acres (bless the mark),
With walls encompassed round—
Where flocks may range and herds may low,
And kids and lambkins play,
And flowers and fruits commingled grow,
All Eden to display.

VI.

I want, when summer's foliage falls,
And autumn strips the trees,
A house within the city's walls,
For comfort and for ease.
But here, as space is somewhat scant,
And acres somewhat rare,
My house in town I only want
To occupy——a square.

VII.

I want a steward, butler, cooks;
　　A coachman, footman, grooms,
A library of well-bound books,
　　And picture-garnished rooms;
Corregios, Magdalen, and Night,
　　The matron of the chair;
Guido's fleet coursers in their flight,
　　And Claudes at least a pair.

VIII.

I want a cabinet profuse
　　Of medals, coins, and gems;
A printing press, for private use,
　　Of fifty thousand ems;
And plants, and minerals, and shells;
　　Worms, insects, fishes, birds;
And every beast on earth that dwells
　　In solitude or herds.

IX.

I want a board of burnished plate,
　　Of silver and of gold;
Tureens of twenty pounds in weight,
　　With sculpture's richest mould;
Plateaus, with chandeliers and lamps,
　　Plates, dishes—all the same;
And porcelain vases, with the stamps
　　Of Sevres, Angouleme.

X.

And maples, of fair glossy stain,
   Must form my chamber doors,
And carpets of the Wilton grain
   Must cover all my floors;
My walls, with tapestry bedeck'd,
   Must never be outdone;
And damask curtains must protect
   Their colors from the sun.

XI.

And mirrors of the largest pane
   From Venice must be brought;
And sandal-wood, and bamboo cane,
   For chairs and tables bought;
On all the mantel-pieces, clocks
   Of thrice-gilt bronze must stand,
And screens of ebony and box
   Invite the stranger's hand.

XII.

I want (who does not want?) a wife,
   Affectionate and fair,
To solace all the woes of life,
   And all its joys to share;
Of temper sweet, of yielding will,
   Of firm, yet placid mind,
With all my faults to love me still,
   With sentiment refin'd.

XIII.

And as Time's car incessant runs,
    And Fortune fills my store,
I want of daughters and of sons
    From eight to half a score.
I want (alas! can mortal dare
    Such bliss on earth to crave?)
That all the girls be chaste and fair—
    The boys all wise and brave.

XIV.

And when my bosom's darling sings,
    With melody divine,
A pedal harp of many strings
    Must with her voice combine.
A piano, exquisitely wrought,
    Must open stand, apart,
That all my daughters may be taught
    To win the stranger's heart.

XV.

My wife and daughters will desire
    Refreshment from perfumes,
Cosmetics for the skin require,
    And artificial blooms.
The civit fragrance shall dispense,
    And treasur'd sweets return;
Cologne revive the flagging sense,
    And smoking amber burn.

XVI.

And when at night my weary head
  Begins to droop and dose,
A southern chamber holds my bed,
  For nature's soft repose;
With blankets, counterpanes, and sheet,
  Mattress, and bed of down,
And comfortables for my feet,
  And pillows for my crown.

XVII.

I want a warm and faithful friend,
  To cheer the adverse hour,
Who ne'er to flatter will descend,
  Nor bend the knee to power;
A friend to chide me when I'm wrong,
  My inmost soul to see;
And that my friendship prove as strong
  For him, as his for me.

XVIII.

I want a kind and tender heart,
  For others' wants to feel;
A soul secure from Fortune's dart,
  And bosom arm'd with steel;
To bear divine chastisement's rod.
  And mingling in my plan,
Submission to the will of God,
  With charity to man.

XIX.

I want a keen, observing eye,
An ever-listening ear,
The truth through all disguise to spy,
And wisdom's voice to hear;
A tongue, to speak at virtue's need,
In Heaven's sublimest strain;
And lips, the cause of man to plead,
And never plead in vain.

XX.

I want uninterrupted health,
Throughout my long career,
And streams of never-failing wealth,
To scatter far and near;
The destitute to clothe and feed,
Free bounty to bestow;
Supply the helpless orphan's need,
And soothe the widow's woe.

XXI.

I want the genius to conceive,
The talents to unfold,
Designs, the vicious to retrieve,
The virtuous to uphold;
Inventive power, combining skill,
A persevering soul,
Of human hearts to mould the will,
And reach from pole to pole.

XXII.

I want the seals of power and place,
  The ensigns of command,
Charged by the people's unbought grace,
  To rule my native land.
Nor crown, nor sceptre would I ask
  But from my country's will,
By day, by night, to ply the task
  Her cup of bliss to fill.

XXIII.

I want the voice of honest praise
  To follow me behind,
And to be thought in future days
  The friend of human kind;
That after ages, as they rise,
  Exulting may proclaim,
In choral union to the skies,
  Their blessings on my name.

XXIV.

These are the wants of mortal man;
  I cannot want them long,
For life itself is but a span,
  And earthly bliss a song.
My last great want, absorbing all,
  Is, when beneath the sod,
And summon'd to my final call,
  The mercy of my God.

XXV.

And oh! while circles in my veins
    Of life the purple stream,
And yet a fragment small remains
    Of nature's transient dream,
My soul, in humble hope unscar'd,
    Forget not thou to pray,
That this thy want may be prepared
    To meet the Judgment Day.

Retrospection

When life's fair dream has passed away
    To three score years and ten,
Before we turn again to clay
    The lot of mortal men,
'Tis wise a backward eye to cast
    On life's revolving scene,
With calmness to review the past
    And ask what we have been.

The cradle and the mother's breast
    Have vanish'd from the mind,
Of joys the sweetest and the best,
    Nor left a trace behind.
Maternal tenderness and care
    Were lavished all in vain—
Of bliss, whatever was our share
    No vestiges remain.

Far distant, like a beacon light
    On ocean's boundless waste,
A single spot appears in sight
    Yet indistinctly traced.
Some mimic stage's thrilling cry,
    Some agony of fear,
Some painted wonder to the eye,
    Some trumpet to the ear.

These are the first events of life
    That fasten on the brain,
And through the world's incessant strife
    Indelible remain.
They form the link with ages past
    From former worlds a gleam;
With murky vapors overcast,
    The net-work of a dream.

To the Sun-Dial,
Under the Window of the Hall of the
House of Representatives of the United States

Thou silent herald of Time's silent flight!
    Say, could'st thou speak, what warning voice were thine?
    Shade, who canst only show how others shine!
Dark, sullen witness of resplendent light
In day's broad glare, and when the moontide bright
    Of laughing fortune sheds the ray divine,
    Thy ready favors cheer us—but decline
The clouds of morning and the gloom of night.
Yet are thy counsels faithful, just, and wise;
    They bid us seize the moments as they pass—
Snatch the retrieveless sunbeam as it flies,
    Nor lose one sand of life's revolving glass—
Aspiring still, with energy sublime,
By virtuous deeds to give eternity to Time.

Version of the One Hundred Seventh Psalm

O that the race of men would raise
 Their voices to their heavenly King,
And with the sacrifice of praise
 The glories of Jehovah sing!—
Ye navigators of the sea,
 Your course on ocean's tides who keep,
And there Jehovah's wonders see,
 His wonders in the briny deep!

He speaks; conflicting whirlwinds fly;
 The waves in swelling torrents flow;
They mount, aspire to heaven on high;
 They sink, as if to hell below:
Their souls with terror melt away;
 They stagger as if drunk with wine
Their skill is vain,—to thee they pray;
 O, save them, Energy divine!

He stays the storm; the waves subside;
 Their hearts with rapture are inspired;
Soft breezes waft them o'er the tide,
 In gladness, to their port desired:
O that mankind the song would raise,
 Jehovah's goodness to proclaim!
Assembled nations shout his praise,
 Assembled elders bless his name!

The Hour-Glass

Alas! how swift the moments fly!
　　How flash the years along!
Scarce here, yet gone already by,
　　The burden of a song.
See childhood, youth, and manhood pass,
　　And age, with furrowed brow;
Time was—Time shall be—drain the glass—
　　But where in Time is *now?*

Time is the measure but of change;
　　No present hour is found;
The past, the future, fill the range
　　Of Time's unceasing round.
Where, then, is *now?* In realms above,
　　With God's atoning Lamb
In regions of eternal love,
　　Where sits enthroned I AM.

Then, pilgrim, let thy joys and tears
　　On Time no longer lean;
But henceforth all thy hopes and fears
　　From earth's affections wean:
To God let votive accents rise;
　　With truth, with virtue, live;
So all the bliss that Time denies
　　Eternity shall give.

Hymn for the Twenty-Second of December

When o'er the billow-heaving deep,
　The fathers of our race,
The precepts of their God to keep,
　Sought here their resting-place—

That gracious God their path prepared,
　Preserved from every harm,
And still for their protection bared
　His everlasting arm.

His breath, inspiring every gale,
　Impels them o'er the main;
His guardian angels spread the sail,
　And tempests howl in vain.

For them old ocean's rocks are smoothed;
　December's face grows mild;
To vernal airs her blasts are soothed,
　And all their rage beguiled.

When Famine rolls her haggard eyes,
　His ever-bounteous hand
Abundance from the sea supplies,
　And treasures from the sand.

Nor yet his tender mercies cease;
　His overruling plan
Inclines to gentleness and peace
　The heart of savage man.

And can our stony bosoms be
  To all these wonders blind?
Nor swell with thankfulness to thee,
  O Parent of mankind?

All-gracious God, inflame our zeal;
  Dispense one blessing more;
Grant us thy boundless love to feel,
  Thy goodness to adore.

Sing to Jehovah a New Song

Sing to Jehovah a new song,
    For deeds of wonder he hath done;
His arm in holiness is strong;
    His hand the victory hath won:
The Lord salvation hath made known;
    His goodness o'er the world extends;
His truth to Israel's house is shown;
    His power to earth's remotest ends.

Shout to Jehovah, all the earth,
    Break forth in joy, exult, and sing;
Let voice, let clarion speak your mirth,
    Trumpet and harp proclaim your King:
Roar, ocean, to thy lowest deep;
    Shout, earth, and all therein that dwell;
Floods, clap your hands as on you sweep:
    Mountains, the choral anthem swell.

Let heaven, and earth, and sea, combine,
    Jehovah's holy name to bless;
Creation owns his power divine,
    The universe his righteousness;
He comes in judgment to display
    Resistless right and boundless grace
The world with equity to sway,
    And blessings shed o'er all our race.

Turn to the Stars of Heaven Thine Eyes

Turn to the stars of heaven thine eyes,
　And God shall meet thee there;
Exalt thy vision to the skies,
　His glory they declare;
Day speaks to day, night teaches night,
　The wonders of their frame,
And all in harmony unite
　Their Maker to proclaim.

Earth has no language, man no speech,
　But gives their voice a tongue;
Their words the world's foundations reach;
　Their hymn in heaven is sung;
Pavilioned there in glory bright,
　As from a blooming bride,
The sun comes forth in floods of light,
　With all a bridegroom's pride.

Glad, like a giant for the race,
　His orient flame ascends,
Soars through the boundless realms of space,
　And in the west descends;
His heat the vital lamp bestows,
　The firmament pervades,
In ocean's darkest caverns glows,
　And earth's profoundest shades.

O Lord My God! How Great Art Thou!

O Lord my God! how great art thou!
    With honor and with glory crowned;
Light's dazzling splendors veil thy brow,
    And gird the universe around.

Spirits and angels thou hast made;
    Thy ministers a flaming fire;
By thee were earth's foundations laid;
    At thy rebuke the floods retire.

Thine are the fountains of the deep;
    By thee their waters swell or fail;
Up to the mountain's summit creep,
    Or shrink beneath the lowly vale.

Thy fingers mark their utmost bound;
    That bound the waters may not pass;
Their moisture swells the teeming ground,
    And paints the valleys o'er with grass.

The waving harvest, Lord, is thine;
    The vineyard, and the olive's juice;
Corn, wine, and oil, by thee combine,
    Life, gladness, beauty, to produce.

The moon for seasons thou hast made,
    The sun for change of day and night;
Of darkness thine the deepest shade,
    And thine the day's meridian light.

O Lord, thy works are all divine;
    In wisdom hast thou made them all;
Earth's teeming multitudes are thine;
    Thine—peopled ocean's great and small.

All these on thee for life depend;
    Thy spirit speaks, and they are born;
They gather what thy bounties send;
    Thy hand of plenty fills the horn.

Thy face is hidden—they turn pale,
    With terror quake, with anguish burn;
Their breath thou givest to the gale;
    They die, and to their dust return.

And thou, my soul, with pure delight,
    Thy voice to bless thy Maker raise;
His praise let morning sing to night,
    And night to morn repeat his praise.

O Lord, Thy All-Discerning Eyes

O Lord, thy all-discerning eyes
  My inmost purpose see;
My deeds, my words, my thoughts, arise
  Alike disclosed to thee:
My sitting down, my rising up,
  Broad noon, and deepest night,
My path, my pillow, and my cup,
  Are open to thy sight.

Before, behind, I meet thine eye,
  And feel thy heavy hand:
Such knowledge is for me too high,
  To reach or understand:
What of thy wonders can I know?
  What of thy purpose see?
Where from thy spirit shall I go?
  Where from thy presence flee?

If I ascend to heaven on high,
  Or make my bed in hell;
Or take the morning's wings, and fly
  O'er ocean's bounds to dwell;
Or seek, from thee, a hiding-place
  Amid the gloom of night—
Alike to thee are time and space,
  The darkness and the light.

For Thee in Zion Waiteth Praise

For thee in Zion waiteth praise,
   O God, O thou that hearest prayer;
To thee the suppliant voice we raise;
   To thee shall all mankind repair.
On thee the ends of earth rely;
   In thee the distant seas confide;
By thee the mountains brave the sky,
   And girded by thy strength abide.

Thou speakest to the tempest peace;
   The roaring wave obeys thy nod;
The tumults of the people cease;
   Earth trembles at the voice of God:
The morning's dawn, the evening's shade,
   Alike thy power with gladness see;
The fields from thee the rains receive,
   And swell with fruitfulness by thee.

Thy river, gracious God, o'erflows;
   Its streams for human wants provide;
At thy command the harvest grows,
   By thy refreshing showers supplied:
Thy bounty clothes the plains with grass;
   Thy path drops fatness as it goes;
And wheresoe'er thy footsteps pass,
   The desert blossoms like the rose.

Thy goodness crowns the circling year;
The wilderness repeats thy voice;
The mountains clad with flocks appear;
The hills on every side rejoice;
And harvests from the valleys spring;
The reaper's sickle they employ;
And, hark! how hill and valley ring
With universal shouts of joy!

My Shepherd Is the Lord on High

My Shepherd is the Lord on high;
  His hand supplies me still;
In pastures green he makes me lie,
  Beside the rippling rill:
He cheers my soul, relieves my woes,
  His glory to display;
The paths of righteousness he shows,
  And leads me in his way.

Though walking through death's dismal shade,
  No evil will I fear;
Thy rod, thy staff shall lend me aid,
  For thou art ever near:
For me a table thou dost spread
  In presence of my foes;
With oil thou dost anoint my head;
  By thee my cup o'erflows.

Thy goodness and thy mercy sure
  Shall bless me all my days;
And I, with lips sincere and pure,
  Will celebrate thy praise.
Yes, in the temple of the Lord
  Forever I will dwell;
To after time thy name record,
  And of thy glory tell.

Send Forth, O God, Thy Truth and Light

Send forth, O God, thy truth and light,
    And let them lead me still,
Undaunted, in the paths of right,
    Up to thy holy hill:
Then to thy altar will I spring,
    And in my God rejoice
And praise shall tune the trembling string,
    And gratitude my voice.

O why, my soul, art thou cast down?
    Within me why distressed?
Thy hopes the God of grace shall crown;
    He yet shall make thee blessed;
To him, my never-failing Friend,
    I bow, and kiss the rod;
To him shall thanks and praise ascend,
    My Saviour and my God.

O Judge Me, Lord, for Thou Art Just

O judge me, Lord, for thou art just;
    Thy statutes are my pride;
In thee alone I put my trust;
    I therefore shall not slide:
O prove me, try my reins and heart;
    Thy mercies, Lord, I know;
I never took the scorner's part,
    Nor with the vain will go.

Of sinners I detest the bands,
    Nor with them will offend;
In innocence will wash my hands,
    And at thine altar bend;
There, with thanksgiving's grateful voice,
    Thy wondrous works will tell;
I love the mansions of thy choice,
    And where thine honors dwell.

Justice
An Ode

I.

Child of the dust! to yonder skies
   Thy vision canst thou turn?
And trace with perishable eyes,
   The seats where seraphs burn?
There, by the throne of God on high,
An angel form canst thou descry,
   Ineffably sublime?
Or is the effulgence of the Light,
Intense, insufferably bright,
   For beings born of Time?

II.

That angel form, in light enshrined,
   Beside the living throne,
Is Justice, still to heaven confined—
   For God is just alone.
This Angel, of celestial birth,
Her faint resemblance here on earth
   Has sent, mankind to guide—
Yet, though obscured her brightest beams,
Still with too vivid ray she gleams
   For Mortals to abide.

III.

When the first father of our race
    Against his God rebelled,
Was banished from his Maker's face,
    From Paradise expelled;
For guilt unbounded to atone,
What bound could punishment have known,
    Had Justice dealt the blow?
Sure, to infernal regions hurled,
His doom had been a flaming world
    Of never ending woe!

IV.

But Mercy, from the throne of God,
    Extended forth her hand;
Withheld th' exterminating rod,
    And quenched the flaming brand:
His blood the blest Redeemer gave,
Th' apostate victim's blood to save,
    And fill redemption's plan:
Angels proclaimed in choral songs,
"Justice to God alone belongs,
    And Mercy pardons man."

V.

When, issuing from the savage wild,
    Man forms the social tie,
Justice severe, and Mercy mild,
    To bind the compact vie;
Of each his own, the parting hedge
Stern Justice takes the solemn pledge;
    The sacred vow enjoins.
While Mercy, with benignant face,
Bids man his fellow-man embrace,
    And heart with heart entwines.

VI.

To both united is the trust
  Of human laws consigned;
One teaches mortals to be just;
  The other, to be kind;
Yet shall not Justice always wear
The garb of punishment, or bear
  The avenging sword to smite:
Nor Mercy's ever gladdening eye
Permit the ruffian to defy
  Th' unerring rule of right.

VII.

To Justice, dearer far the part
  To tune the plausive voice;
Of Virtue to delight the heart,
  And bid the good rejoice.
To yield the meed of grateful praise—
The deathless monument to raise,
  To honor Virtue dead;
Or wreathe the chaplet of renown,
The laurel or the mural crown,
  For living Virtue's head.

VIII.

Here, to defend his native land,
  His sword the patriot draws;
Here the mock hero lifts his hand
  To aid a tyrant's cause.
When, meeting on the field of blood
They pour the sanguinary flood,
  Whose triumph waves unfurled?
Alas! let Cheronea tell;
Or plains where godlike Brutus fell,
  Or Cæsar won the world!

IX.

In arms, when hostile nations rise
     And blood the strife decides,
'Tis brutal force awards the prize,
     Her head while Justice hides.
But short is force's triumph base:
Justice unveils her awful face,
     And hurls him from the steep;
Stripe from his brow the wreath of fame,
And after ages load his name
     With curses load and deep.

X.

Behold the lettered sage devote
     The labors of his mind,
His country's welfare to promote.
     And benefit mankind.
Lo! from the blackest caves of hell,
A phalanx fierce of monsters fell,
     Combine their fearful bands—
Hit fame asperse, his toils assail;
Till Justice holds aloft her scale
     And shields him from their hands.

XI.

Of excellence, in every clime,
     'Tis thus the lot is cast;
Passion usurps the present time,
     But Justice rules the past:
Envy, and selfishness, and pride,
The passing hours of man divide
     With unresisted sway;
But Justice comes, with noiseless tread,
O'ertakes the filmy spider's thread
     And sweeps the net away.

XII.

Eternal Spirit! Lord supreme
  Of blessing and of woe!
Of Justice, ever living stream!
  Whose mercies ceaseless flow—
Make me, while earth shall be my span,
Just to my fellow-mortal, man,
  Whate'er my lot may be.
And when this transient scene is o'er,
Pure let my deathless spirit soar,
  And Mercy find from thee.

To Sally

"Integer vitæ, scelerisque purus
Non eget Mauris jaculis, neque arcu."

The man in righteousness array'd,
    A pure and blameless liver,
Needs not the keen Toledo blade,
    Nor venom-freighted quiver.
What though he wind his toilsome way
    O'er regions wild and weary—
Through Zara's burning desert stray;
    Or Asia's jungles dreary:

What though he plough the billowy deep
    By lunar light, or solar,
Meet the resistless Simoon's sweep,
    Or iceberg circumpolar.
In bog or quagmire deep and dank,
    His foot shall never settle;
He mounts the summit of Mont Blanc,
    Or Popocatepetl.

On Chimborazo's breathless height,
    He treads o'er burning lava;
Or snuffs the Bohan Upas blight,
    The deathful plant of Java.
Through every peril he shall pass,
    By Virtue's shield protected;
And still by Truth's unerring glass
    His path shall be directed.

Else wherefore was it, Thursday last,
 While strolling down the valley
Defenceless, musing as I pass'd
 A canzonet to Sally;
A wolf, with mouth protruding snout,
 Forth from the thicket bounded—
I clapped my hands and raised a shout—
 He heard—and fled—confounded.

Tangier nor Tunis never bred
 An animal more crabbed;
Nor Fez, dry nurse of lions, fed
 A monster half so rabid.
Nor Ararat so fierce a beast
 Has seen, since days of Noah;
Nor strong, more eager for a feast,
 The fell constrictor boa.

Oh! place me where the solar beam
 Has scorch'd all verdure vernal;
Or on the polar verge extreme,
 Block'd up with ice eternal—
Still shall my voice's tender lays
 Of love remain unbroken;
And still my charming Sally praise,
 Sweet smiling and sweet spoken.

To a Lady
Who Presented Him a Pair of Knit Gloves

Who shall say that public life
Is nothing but discordant strife?
And he whose heart is tuned to love,
Tender and gentle as the dove,
Must whet his talons, night and day,
For conflicts with the birds of prey?

This world is fashioned, Lady fair,
Of Joy and Sorrow, Ease and Care;
Of sudden changes, small and great;
Of upward and of downward fate:
And whoso bends his mood to trace
The annals of man's fallen race,
May sigh to find that nature's plan
Is ruthless war from man to man.
But nature, cruel to be kind,
Not to war only man consigned;
But gave him woman on the spot,
To mingle pleasure in his lot:
That if with man war cannot cease,
With woman reigns eternal peace.

Fair Lady, I have lived on earth
Nigh fourscore summers from my birth;
And half the sorrows I have felt
Have by my brother man been dealt;
And all the ills I have endured
By man inflicted, woman cured.
The glove from man to man, thou know'st,
Of fierce defiance is the boast;
And cast in anger on the floor,
To mortal combat shows the door:
But gloves from woman's gentle hand,
Of cordial Friendship bear the wand;
And in return a single glove
Betokens emblematic Love.

Thy gift, fair Ellen, then I take,
And cherish for the giver's sake;
And while they shelter from the storm
My hands, the heart alike shall warm;
And speed for thee to God above,
The fervid prayer of faithful love.

The Lip and the Heart

One day between the Lip and the Heart
    A wordless strife arose,
Which was expertest in the art
    His purpose to disclose.

The Lip called forth the vassal Tongue,
    And made him vouch—a lie!
The slave his servile anthem sung,
    And brav'd the listening sky.

The Heart to speak in vain essay'd,
    Nor could his purpose reach—
His will nor voice nor tongue obeyed,
    His silence was his speech.

Mark thou their difference, child of earth!
    While each performs his part,
Not all the lip can speak is worth
    The silence of the heart.

Written in an Album

In days of yore, the poet's pen
    From wing of bird was plundered;
Perhaps of goose, but, now and then,
    From Jove's own eagle sundered.
But now metallic pens disclose
    Alone the poet's numbers
In iron inspiration glows,
    Or with the minstrel slumbers.

Fair damsel! could my pen impart,
    In prose or lofty rhyme,
The pure emotions of my heart,
    To speed the flight of time;
What metal from the womb of earth
    Could worth intrinsic bear,
To stamp with corresponding worth
    The blessings thou shouldst share?

A Theory of Comets
To the Comet Seen at Quincy, 6. October 1825
A Sonnet

Portentous stranger, from a world unknown!
    Short visitant from realms of boundless space,
    Oh! say shall man be never taught to trace
Thy path immense around the solar throne—
Art thou to mortal vision only shown,
    To glare, the fear and wonder of our race
    To flash, and flit across the walking face—
Then traverse the void infinite alone?
Methinks thou art the spectre of a star.
    An orb deceas'd, and disenthralled of clay
In light, refin'd from elemental War,
    And bound to regions of eternal day.
Cease, soul presumptuous, and enquire no more;
But, silent, Him who made these countless worlds, adore.

On Witnessing the Ascension in a Balloon of Madame Johnson, a Widowed Mother, at Castle Garden, New York, 20. October 1825
A Sonnet

Lo! she ascends! aloft in air she flies!
  Borne on the pinions of the wintry blast—
  She seems as one, whose days on earth are past—
A sainted seraph, soaring to the skies.
Still she recedes, and still my straining eyes,
  Intent upon the dwindling orb are cast.
  Tis gone—Perchance this moment is her last!
And oh! what pangs within my bosom rise!
Those puffed cheeks, those agonizing hearts
  Of children to the world's cold bounty left;
For whom, of Death, she dares the direst darts;
  Oh who shall shield them, of her cares bereft?—
All gracious God! to land her safe from harm
Extend beneath her car, thine everlasting arm.

Day of my father's birth, I hail thee yet.
What though his body moulders in the grave,
Yet shall not Death th' immortal soul enslave;
The sun is not extinct—his orb has set.
And where on earth's wide ball shall man be met,
While time shall run, but from thy spirit brave
Shall learn to grasp the boon his Maker gave,
And spurn the terror of a tyrant's threat?
Who but shall learn that freedom is the prize
Man still is bound to rescue or maintain;
That nature's God commands the slave to rise,
And on the oppressor's head to break his chain.
Roll, years of promise, rapidly roll round,
Till not a slave shall on this earth be found!

John Tyler

1790–1862

∽

10ᵗʰ president (1841–45)

John Tyler was the first vice president to get a promotion when the president passed away. He vetoed a banking bill supported by his party, which led all but one member of his Cabinet to resign.

Tyler wrote poetry before, during, and after his presidency. He mostly kept his verse private for himself and his family. According to the Library of Congress's "Presidents as Poets," "While Tyler's poetry went unseen and unheard among most outsiders, it featured . . . in his private life as a source of consolation, reflection, and delight."

In his poignant elegy, "Oh child of my love thou wert born for a day," Tyler mourns his daughter Anne Contesse, who died at three months old in 1825. Tyler recalls that she was "lovely" throughout her short life and looks forward to seeing her face again.

Tyler's only poem associated with a moment in his political career is "Speed On, My Vessel." He wrote it in 1836 after resigning from the Senate, looking forward to a happy retirement from public service, at least in the short term.

After Tyler's first wife, Letitia, died, he wooed his second wife, Julia, who was thirty years his junior. Prior to becoming the first president to get married while in office in 1844, he wrote two poems as part of his courtship. In *And Tyler Too*, Robert Seager II explained that Tyler was smitten with Julia's "beauty, vivacity, good humor, and poise" and that when he "was happy, poetry invariably flowed from his lips and from his pen." He penned "Sweet Lady, Awake!" in 1843 and revised it during their honeymoon, and Julia set it to music. In "Shall I again that Harp unstring," Tyler notes that he has sung and played music—metaphorically, loved—before and he looks to do so again. Tyler composed the poem in Julia's autograph album, which had a wider audience than he anticipated. Upon seeing the album, Supreme Court Justice Henry Baldwin shared the poem, leading to gossip about Tyler's intention to remarry in Washington political circles.

Tyler wrote "Virginia," a tribute to the state where he had been governor, in 1848. His daughter Letitia Tyler Semple, who handled First Lady duties prior to his second marriage, set "Virginia" to music and sung it.

Tyler penned "To M. G. B." for Margaret Gardiner Beeckman, Julia's sister, in 1852, after her family moved to Staten Island. That is the "Isle" referred to throughout the poem.

Oh child of my love thou wert born for a day
And like morning's vision have vanished away
Thine eye scarce had ope'd on the world's beaming light
Ere 'twas seal'd up in death and envelop'd in night

Oh child of my love as a beautiful flower
Thy blossom expanded a short fleeting hour
The winter of death hath blighted thy bloom
And thou lyest alone in the cold dreary tomb

Oh child of my love no mother's fond care
Can nurse thee or sing thee thy lullaby there
Thy cradle is lonely, thy dwelling is low
No father or mother can wait on thee now

Thou wert lovely my baby most beauteous and fair
Than the wealth of the world, to thy parents more dear
Through pain and distress; yes to thy last breath
Thou wert lovely dear baby e'en lovely in death

Oh child of my love the day will arrive
When thy grave shall be riven and thou shalt revive
When thy father shall gaze on thy beautiful face
And thou shalt be clasp'd in thy mother's embrace

Then sleep on my infant thy dwelling is low
But minist'ring angels attend on thee now
Thy spirit already has gone to its rest
My child now an angel resides with the bless'd

Speed On, My Vessel

Air—"Oh no! I'll never mention him."

Speed on, my vessel, speed thee fast,
  Swift o'er the briny sea;
I am going to my home at last,
  Where there's peace and rest for me.

My bark of life, long tempest tossed,
  Seeks now a place of rest,
Where memory of the past is lost,
  And sunshine fills my breast.

Now, at the harbor's open gate,
  The anxious eyes are strained;
The "wee ones" all will set up late,
  And sigh for me detained.

Then on, my vessel, speed thee fast,
  Swift o'er the briny sea;
Home rises on my sight at last,
  And *there* is rest for me.

Sweet Lady, Awake!
A Serenade Dedicated to Miss Julia Gardiner

Sweet lady awake, from your slumbers awake,
Weird beings we come o'er hill and through brake
To sing you a song in the stillness of night,
Oh, read you our riddle fair lady aright?
We are sent by the one whose fond heart is your own,
Who mourns in thy absence and sighs all alone.
Alas, he is distant—but tho' far, far away,
He thinks of you, lady, by night and by day.
    Sweet lady awake, sweet lady awake!

His hearth, altho' lonely, is bright with your fame,
And therefore we breathe not the breath of his name.
For oh! if your dreams have response in your tone,
Long since have you known it as well as your own.
We are things of the sea, of the earth, and the air,
But ere you again to your pillow repair,
Entrust us to say you gave ear to our strain,
And were *he* the minstrel you would listen again.
    Sweet lady awake, sweet lady awake!

Shall I again that Harp unstring,
Which long hath been a useless thing,
Unheard in Lady's bower?
Its notes were once full wild and free,
When I, to one as fair as thee,
Did sing in youth's bright hours.
Like to those raven tresses, gay,
Which o'er thy ivory shoulders play,
Were those which waked my lyre.
Eyes like to thine, which beamed as bright
As stars, that through the veil of night,
Sent forth a brimy fire.
I seize the Harp; alas! in vain,
I try to wake those notes again,
Which it breathed forth of yore.
With youth its sound has died away:
Old age hath touch'd it with decay;
It will be *heard* no more!
Yet, at my touch, that ancient lyre
Deigns one parting note respire.
Lady, it breathes of heaven.
It speaks in praise of holy shrine;
Of eyes upturned to Him divine,
By whom are sins forgiven.

II.

It tells the rose, which blooms so gay
And courts the Zyphers kiss today,
As if t'would never die;
Its leaves, which perfume all around,
Strew'd on the earth shall soon be found;
Unnoticed, there to die.

Unwelcome truth it tells to thee,
Lovely in Beauty's majesty,
The roses fate—is thine:
Unlike in this—thy soul, so pure,
Through endless ages shall endure.
Kneel thou at Holy Shrines!

Virginia

My native land, my native land,
Whether thy frown or smile I see
Still by thy banner will I stand,
Wave it o'er land or sea:
Ne'er can I thy sweet name forget
Thy role of patriots hoary
Whose fame undying ne'er shall set
But shine in light and glory—
    Oh! Oh! Oh!

[Chorus]
My native land, my native land,
My heart shall ever turn to thee.
Fain would I shout from hill and strand
That name so dear to me—
Oh! Virginia, proud Virginia!
My native land, I love by thee.

II.
Land of the wise and nobly brave,
Thy glorious star resplendent shines,
E'en now across the distant wave
From Aztec's golden mine—
Thy war-cry still is heard above
The din of battles roar,
Thy sons lead on the gallant hosts,
For victory as of yore
    Oh! Oh! Oh!

III.

Though age thy regal brow has scarred
No touch of Time can dim thy fame,
Thy dreams and valleys mountain barred
Eternal strength proclaim.
Proud mother state, on whose broad breast
Was cradled Liberty.
Within thy arms oh may I rest;
And live and die for thee.
    Oh! Oh! Oh!

To M. G. B.

The springtime has its violet
The summer has its rose
The autumn has its varied tints
The winter has its snows—
    But springtime's violet, summer's rose
    Are not so sweet to see
    Or autumn's tints, or winter's snows
    So bright, so pure as she
        As Margaret of the lonely Isle
        That is girt in by the sea.

I wandered on the Ocean's shore
And with its pebbles play'd
By Mountain's stream where Eagle's soar
In early sunlight stray'd
    But Ocean's depths do not contain
    A gem can match her eye
    Nor Mountain's streamlet's dimpled laugh
    With her bright smile can vie
        There's naught can match the radiant smile
        Of Margaret of the Isle.

In her light form a magic lies
And in her shining hair
There's magic in her beaming eyes
And in her graceful air
    And I will worship at her feet
    And live in her bright smile
    With my last sigh the name repeat
    Of Margaret of the Isle
        Dear Margaret of the lonely Isle
        That is girt in by the sea.

Abraham Lincoln

1809–65

◇

16th president (1861–65)

Abraham Lincoln led the nation to victory during the Civil War and declared that all slaves were free. As a writer, he is remembered for his masterful prose, including *The Lincoln-Douglas Debates*, his inaugurals, and the Gettysburg Address.

Other than the two presidents who published books of poetry, Lincoln was probably the most prolific poet. A few publishers have released slim volumes of his verse. Several sources posited that the primary value of Lincoln's poetry is explaining the poetic flourishes in his prose. In *Lincoln: The Biography of a Writer*, Fred Kaplan hailed Lincoln as the president who best used "language as an agent of consensus and persuasion to shape the national will." According to Kaplan, Lincoln excelled as a writer because of his "feel for poetic language, for the right word in the right place . . . for the pithy language that reveals human nature and the elevated language that evokes human ideals."

After developing an interest in poetry around age twelve, Lincoln was an avid reader of a wide range of poets for the rest of his life. He memorized entire poems and excerpts and recited them. As president, he sometimes woke up after midnight and walked around the White House discussing poetry he had recently read, his secretary recalled.

Lincoln wrote this chapter's first three selections in his arithmetic book when he was between fifteen and seventeen. Some scholars speculate that he copied parts from other sources. The two quatrains might lack substance, but they give an early glimpse into his sense of humor and self-confidence.

The next trio, from 1846–47, is Lincoln's longest and most significant poetry. His 1844 visit to Indiana, where he had grown up, inspired him to reflect on his childhood in these autobiographical poems. Kaplan noted that Lincoln used the exercise for "self-exploration and pleasurable expression," praising his "skill with meter, rhyme, and word choice" as well as his sincerity. "My Childhood-Home I See Again" reminisces bittersweetly about his youth and loved ones who are no longer alive. "The Maniac"—a term that suggested losing mental faculties and control of one's actions—addresses a schoolmate whom he saw upon returning to Indiana. "The Bear Hunt" comically recounts a hunting party's pursuit of prey and their disagreement over who killed a bear, which Lincoln, an attorney, likens to how lawyers "*argufy*" in a murder trial. He sent the poems to a friend and asked that they be published anonymously, saying that the "risk" of "being ridiculed for having written them" outweighed any potential reward. He discussed composing a fourth poem in the series, but if he followed through, it is not extant.

The penultimate selection is from 1858. It is one of two poems that Lincoln penned for the daughters of the proprietor of a hotel while staying there.

He composed the final poem following the Union's victory at the Battle of Gettysburg in 1863. Written in the voice of Robert E. Lee, the colloquial poem mocks Lee and the Confederacy.

Abraham Lincoln
his hand and pen
he will be good but
god knows When.

Abraham Lincoln is my name
And with my pen I wrote the same,
I wrote in both haste and speed
And left it here for fools to read.

"Time! what an empty vapor 'tis!
And days how swift they are!
Swift as an Indian arrow,
Fly on like a shooting-star.
The present moment just is here,
Then slide away in haste,
That we can never say they're ours,
But only say they are past."

My Childhood-Home I See Again

My childhood's home I see again,
  And sadden with the view;
And still, as memory crowds my brain,
  There's pleasure in it too.

O Memory! thou midway world
  'Twixt earth and paradise,
Where things decayed and loved ones lost
  In dreamy shadows rise,

And, freed from all that's earthly vile,
  Seen hallowed, pure, and bright,
Like scenes in some enchanted isle
  All bathed in liquid light.

As dusky mountains please the eye
  When twilight chases day;
As bugle-notes, that, passing by,
  In distance die away;

As leaving some grand waterfall,
  We, lingering, list its roar—
So memory will hallow all
  We've known, but know no more.

Near twenty years have passed away
  Since here I bid farewell
To woods and fields, and scenes of play,
  And playmates loved so well.

Where many were, but few remain
 Of old familiar things;
But seeing them, to mind again
 The lost and absent brings.

The friends I left that parting day,
 How changed, as time has sped!
Young childhood grown, strong manhood gray,
 And half of all are dead.

I hear the loved survivors tell,
 How naught from death could save,
Till every sound appears a knell,
 And every spot a grave.

I range the fields with pensive tread,
 And pace the hollow rooms,
And feel (companion of the dead)
 I'm living in the tombs.

The Maniac

But here's an object more of dread
    Than aught the grave contains—
A human form with reason fled,
    While wretched life remains.

When terror spread, and neighbors ran
    Your dangerous strength to bind,
And soon, a howling, crazy man,
    Your limbs were fast confined:

How then you strove and shrieked aloud,
    Your bones and sinews bared;
And fiendish on the gazing crowd
    With burning eyeballs glared;

And begged and swore, and wept and prayed,
    With maniac laughter joined!
How fearful were these signs displayed
    By pangs that killed the mind!

And when at length the drear and long
    Time soothe thy fiercer woes,
How plaintively thy mournful song
    Upon the still night rose!

I've heard it oft as if I dreamed,
    Far distant, sweet and lone,
The funeral dirge it ever seemed
    Of reason dead and gone.

To drink its strains I've stole away,
  All stealthily and still,
Ere yet the rising god of day
  Had streaked the eastern hill.

Air held her breath; trees with the spell
  Seemed sorrowing angels round,
Whose swelling tears in dewdrops fell
  Upon the listening ground.

But this is past, and naught remains
  That raised thee o'er the brute;
Thy piercing shrieks and soothing strain
  Are like, forever mute.

Now fare thee well! More thou the cause
  Than subject now of woe.
All mental pangs by time's kind laws
  Hast lost the power to know.

O death! thou awe-inspiring prince
  That keepst the world in fear,
Why dost thou tear more blest ones hence,
  And leave him lingering here?

The Bear Hunt

A wild bear chase didst never see?
    Then hast thou lived in vain—
Thy richest bump of glorious glee
    Lies desert in thy brain.

When first my father settled here,
    'Twas then the frontier line;
The panther's scream filled night with fear
    And bears preyed on the swine.

But woe for bruin's short-lived fun
    When rose the squealing cry;
Now man and horse, with dog and gun
    For vengeance at him fly.

A sound of danger strikes his ear;
    He gives the breeze a snuff;
Away he bounds, with little fear,
    And seeks the tangled *rough*.

On press his foes, and reach the ground
    Where's left his half-munched meal;
The dogs, in circles, scent around
    And find his fresh made trail.

With instant cry, away they dash,
    And men as fast pursue;
O'er logs they leap, through water splash
    And shout the brisk halloo.

Now to elude the eager pack
    Bear shuns the open ground,
Through matted vines he shapes his track,
    And runs it, round and round.

The tall, fleet cur, with deep-mouthed voice
    Now speeds him, as the wind;
While half-grown pup, and short-legged fice
    Are yelping far behind.

And fresh recruits are dropping in
    To join the merry corps;
With yelp and yell, a mingled din—
    The woods are in a roar—

And round, and round the chase now goes,
    The world's alive with fun;
Nick Carter's horse his rider throws,
    And Mose Hills drops his gun.

Now, sorely pressed, bear glances back,
    And lolls his tired tongue,
When as, to force him from his track
    An ambush on him sprung.

Across the glade he sweeps for flight,
    And fully is in view—
The dogs, new fired by the sight
    Their cry and speed renew.

The foremost ones now reach his rear;
    He turns, they dash away,
And circling now the wrathful bear
    They have him full at bay.

At top of speed the horsemen come,
  All screaming in a row—
"Whoop!" "Take him, Tiger!" "Seize him, Drum!"
  Bang—bang! the rifles go!

And furious now, the dogs he tears,
  And crushes in his ire—
Wheels right and left, and upward rears,
  With eyes of burning fire.

But leaden death is at his heart—
  Vain all the strength he plies,
And, spouting blood from every part,
  He reels, and sinks, and dies!

And now a dinsome clamor rose,—
  "But who should have his skin?"
Who first draws blood, each hunter knows
  This prize must always win.

But, who did this, and how to trace
  What's true from what's a lie,—
Like lawyers in a murder case
  They stoutly *argufy.*

Aforesaid fice, of blustering mood,
  Behind, and quite forgot,
Just now emerging from the wood
  Arrives upon the spot,

With grinning teeth, and up-turned hair
  Brim full of spunk and wrath,
He growls, and seizes on dead bear
  And shakes for life and death—

And swells, as if his skin would tear,
    And growls, and shakes again,
And swears, as plain as dog can swear
    That he has won the skin!

Conceited whelp! we laugh at thee,
    Nor mind that not a few
Of pompous, two-legged dogs there be
    Conceited quite as you.

To Linnie

A sweet plaintive song did I hear
And I fancied that she was the singer.
May emotions as pure as that song set astir
Be the wont that the future shall bring her.

Gen. Lee's Invasion of the North, Written by Himself—

"In eighteen sixty three, with pomp,
  and mighty swell,
Me and Jeff's Confederacy, went
  forth to sack Phil. del.
The Yankees they got arter us, and
  gin us partic'lar h_ll,
And we skedaddled back again,
  and didn't sack Phil. del."

Ulysses S. Grant

1822–85

~~~

18ᵗʰ president (1869–77)

Ulysses S. Grant was a revered war hero who commanded the Union armies during the Civil War. As president, he worked to move the nation past the remnants of slavery during Reconstruction. He issued a proclamation that solidified the eight-hour workday for federal employees, and he signed legislation making Yellowstone the first national park.

Grant's bona fides as a writer are impeccable. In *Author in Chief,* Craig Fehrman dubbed Grant "the presidency's greatest memoirist." Mark Twain referred to Grant's *Personal Memoirs* as a "literary masterpiece," and historian Ron Chernow called it "probably the foremost military memoir in the English language."

Whether Grant was a poet is less certain. He supposedly wrote an acrostic in 1839, when he was seventeen, before attending the US Military Academy at West Point. The poem spells out the name of Mary King, his romantic interest. Grant affirms his military aspirations and asks King to remember him when he is away. While the poem is widely attributed to Grant, its authorship is not definitive. One theory posits that he penned the first couplet and his sister wrote the rest.

My country calls and I obey,
And shortly I'll be on my way,
Removed from home far in the West,
Yet you with home and friends are blest.

Kindly then remember me.
I'll also often think of thee,
Nor forget the soldier story,
Gone to gain the field of glory.

James Abram Garfield

1831–81

◦◦◦

20ᵗʰ president (1881)

James Abram Garfield was a teacher, the president of Western Reserve Eclectic Institute (later Hiram College), an ordained minister, a major general during the Civil War, and a nine-term congressman. He served as president of the US for only four months before being shot, and he died two months later.

After he passed away, Richard Salter Storrs compiled *In Memoriam: Gems of Poetry and Song on James A. Garfield* and included two poems by Garfield. According to Storrs, they "show something of his poetic inspiration, as well as his broad native gifts and consummate culture." Garfield penned "Autumn" while he was a student at Williams College, and Storrs hailed it as "singularly touching, embracing with comprehensive sympathy his love for the beautiful and harmonious in nature." Garfield composed "Memory" before his first term in Congress.

The final three selections appear in Corydon E. Fuller's *Reminiscences of James A. Garfield.* When he was a teacher, Garfield interpolated a two-stanza poem in a letter to Fuller. In "Sam," Garfield is critical of the Know-Nothing Party, nicknamed Sam. This nativist political movement, which opposed immigrants and the Catholic Church, had its heyday in the 1850s. Fuller opined that some lines in "To Hattie," which Garfield wrote in Great Barrington, Massachusetts, "would do no discredit to the genius of any poet of the last century." Fuller added that "very frequently there appears a rich vein of poetic thought and expression in [Garfield's] prose writings which is far beyond the reach of many who have been ranked as poets."

Autumn

Old Autumn thou art here! Upon the earth
And in the heavens the signs of death are hung;
For o'er the earth's brown breast stalks pale decay,
And 'mong the lowering clouds the wild winds wail,
And sighing sadly, shout the solemn dirge
O'er summer's fairest flowers, all faded now.
The winter god, descending from the skies,
Has reached the mountain tops and decked their brows
With glittering frosty crowns, and breathed his breath
Among the trumpet pines, that herald forth
His coming.

                  Before the driving blast
The mountain oak bows down his hoary head,
And flings his withered locks to the rough gales
That fiercely roar among his branches bare,
Uplifted to the dark, unpitying heavens.
The skies have put their mourning garments on,
And hung their funeral drapery on the clouds.
Dead nature soon will wear her shrouds of snow,
And lie entombed in winter's icy grave.

Thus passes life. As heavy age comes on,
The joys of youth—bright beauties of the spring—
Grow dim and faded, and the long dark night
Of death's chill winter comes. But as the spring
Rebuilds the ruined wrecks of winter's waste,
And cheers the gloomy earth with joyous light
So o'er the tomb the star of hope shall rise
And usher in an ever-during day.

Memory

'Tis beauteous night! the stars look brightly down
Upon the earth, decked in her robe of snow.
No light gleams at the window, save my own,
Which gives its cheer to midnight and to me.
And now, with noiseless step, sweet memory comes
And leads me gently through her twilight realms.
What poet's tuneful lyre has ever sung
Or delicate pen e'er portrayed,
The enchanted, shadowy land where memory dwells?
It has its valleys, cheerless, lone and drear,
Dark-shaded by the mournful cypress tree;

And yet its sun-lit mountain-tops are bathed
In Heaven's own blue. Upon its craggy cliffs,
Robed in the distant light of dreamy years,
Are clustered joys serene of other days.
Upon its gentle, sloping hillsides bend
The weeping willows o'er the sacred dust
Of dear departed ones! yet in that land,
Where'er our footsteps fall upon the shore,
They that were sleeping rise from out the dust
Of death's long, silent years, and round us stand
As erst they did before the prison tomb
Received their clay within its voiceless halls.
The heavens that bend above that land are hung
With clouds of various hues. Some dark and chill,
Surcharged with sorrow, cast with somber shade
Upon the sunny, joyous land below.
Others are floating through the dreamy air,
White as the falling snow, their margins tinged
With gold and crimsoned hues; their shadows fall

Upon the flowery meads and sunny slopes,
Soft as the shadow of an angel's wing.
When the rough battle of the day is done,
And evening's peace falls gently on the heart.
I bound away across the noisy years,
Unto the utmost verge of memory's land,
Where earth and sky in dreamy distance meet,
And memory dim with dark oblivion joins,
Where woke the first remembered sounds that fell

Upon the ear in childhood's early morn;
And, wandering thence along the rolling years,
I see the shadow of my former self
Gliding from childhood up to man's estate.
The path of youth winds down through many a vale,
And on the brink of many a dread abyss,
From out whose darkness comes no ray of light,
Save that a phantom dances o'er the gulf
And beckons toward the verge. Again the path
Leads o'er the summit where the sunbeams fall;
And thus in light and shade, sunshine and gloom,
Sorrow and joy, the life-path leads along.

Of all the trades by men pursued
    There's none that's more perplexing
Than is the country pedagogue's—
    It's every way most vexing.

Cooped in a little narrow cell,
    As hot as black Tartarus,
As well in Pandemonium dwell
    As in this little school house.

Sam

We sing no more in lofty classic strain,
Of gods and heroes, demigods and war,
Nor soar above the clouds and 'mong the stars,
Extol the grandeur of the rolling orbs.
Nor ride we more upon the cloudy car
Along the threat'ning heavens 'mid the murky storms,
Where the deep thunder rolls and lightning plays;
Nor revel in the fairy land of dreams,
Where crystal rivers murmuring roll along
O'er sands of gold and sparkling diamond stones.
An *earthly* theme be ours to sing in humble verse,
The *wonder of our age—Immortal Sam.*

'T was noon of night, and by his flickering lamp
That floated o'er his dingy room and damp,
With glassy eye and haggard face there sat
A disappointed worn out Democrat.
His eloquence all wasted—plans all failed,
His spurious coin fast to the counter nailed.

Deception's self was now at length deceived;
His lies political, no more believed.
Fair type was he of many Solons more,
Whose bodies politic lie rotting on the shore,
Needing *one Free Soil gift,* at least some friendly clay
To hide the unburied corpse from light of day.
At length he rose in haste, "I have it now,"
(A smile of joy lit up his darkened brow,)
"The people cast me off, I'll raise a storm,
I'll stir the nation with the cry 'Reform,'

I'll tell them treason floats on every breeze,
And danger whispers in the sighing trees.
I'll call them gallant heroes, patriots, braves,
Defenders of their homes, their fathers' graves!
Me, they shall call the nation's savior then;
Then gold and office shall be mine again."
He gathered round him many of his kind,
Waste lumber, by all parties left behind.
They sat that night in council, and at morn,
When all the stars grew dim, then "*Sam*" was born.
Illustrious son of more illustrious sires!
How glowed within his heart the patriotic fires!
What love he cherished for the sacred cause
Of the *Dear People* and their fathers' laws!

The alarm was sounded; over hill and dale,
It flew upon the wings of every gale;
The granite mountains heard it, and the plains
Of the wild West caught the awakening strains.
Freedom in peril! the great crisis comes!
Arouse, ye millions! beat the signal drums!
Vengeance upon the mercenary brood
Of papal minions, pouring like a flood
Over fair Freedom's land, the Freeman's home!
Behold the swarming thousands as they come!
From lip to lip, the startling rumor flies,
With ears erect and wide distended eyes,
All eager listen to the growing tale,
Which gains new terror from each passing gale.
The sturdy yeoman, in his midnight dream,
Saw the red flag of war, the saber's gleam.

Heard the loud death shriek, saw the assassin's stroke,
The pious layman saw in visions dire
The Inquisitorial rack, the martyr's fire,
Pale ghosts went trooping up the midnight sky,
Beck'ning with shadowy hands to raise the warning cry.

The cry was raised, the people's voice went forth;
From Sacramento's sands to the far North,
Sam's army mustered. Bold to war they go,
To fight, how manfully! their phantom foe.
And Massachusetts, puritanic State,
Whose very *smiles* are *solemn*, was not late
In sending forth the sons of pilgrim sires
To lift on high the Salem broom, and light again the fires,
"War, to the knife," they cry, "on popery!
No foreigner oppressed shall hither flee;
Drive back the poor to homeless misery,
Who left the tyrant's land beyond the sea.
Down with the papal church nor heed its loss,
The stars and stripes shall wave above the cross!"
The storm grew darker; like a foaming tide,
That drinks the mountain torrent in from either side.
So grew the people's wrath, which, with resistless force
Swept down all party lines in its swift course,
And tossing on the foam-capped waves were seen
The struggling forms of what had lately been
Whigs, Democrats, Barnburners, Silver Greys,
Exploded fragments of other days.

The *lightest* floated foremost, the least known
Rode into office, while the old sank down.
And he, the Æolus, who raised the storm,
Our quondam Democrat, sank down forlorn,
With all his motley crew; there still they sleep,
And 'mong their bones the slimy monsters creep.
Sam's aspirations grew; he longed to gain
Nebraska's wood crowned hight and Kansas' plains,
The rolling prairie, broad and wild and free,
An ocean of sweet flowers, a waving sea
Of verdure spread; from out its hallowed soil
He'd wring vile gold, bought by the bondsman's toil.

For this foul end be sent the summons forth
To all his legions in the South and North,
To meet in solemn conclave and prepare
Fetters for millions yet unborn to wear.
Unhappy Sam! that was his fatal day,
When 'gainst the slave his power he did array;
When on the hands outstretched, imploring aid,
He would have bound the chains himself had made.
Freemen then saw beneath his robe of light,
A fiend incarnate from the realms of night.
That was the rock on which the millions dashed,
And as a wave to foaming fury lashed,
Thunders its rage against the rock-bound shore,
Then roll away and with a sullen roar
Seeks its deep ocean waves; his gathered band
Poured murmuring away and on the strand,
Left *him*, in all his vileness there to lie,
Where *yet* he *gasps*, refusing still to die.

To Hattie

The western sun had sought his ocean bed
Behind the granite hills, and sable night
Had spread her raven wing wide o'er the world,
When first I gazed upon the evening star
From this, the lovely village where perchance
Thy home is, Hattie, though I know it not,
Nor thee. But as the rosy-fingered dawn
Doth ope the gates of morn, and paint a blush
Of crimson hue upon the Day-God's brow,
At which the child of nature loves to gaze,
So in the "*Courier*" *of* yesternight
The golden glories of a "Berkshire Morn"
Thou didst, in glowing verse, to me portray
Ere I beheld it; and no fairer is
The scene that I this early morning view,
Than was the picture which you drew,
                                    But yet
Where'er is home, sweet home, there beauty is.
My native State! I love thy welcome name,
Ohio. 'T is a word that echoes back
The names of mother, sister, brother, friends,
And all that clings so fondly to the heart.
It speaks of home, of boyhood's happy years,
Of days long buried with the solemn past;
Of scenes, bright, joyous scenes, now gone for aye,
But graved in gold on Memory's faithful page.
It calls companions from their graveyard homes
To look on me as they were wont, before
The dark and voiceless tomb o'er them had closed
Its sombre portal, and had left the worm
To riot on their loved but mouldering hearts.

Beloved spot, where first I breathed the air
Of heaven, and looked upon the morning sun,
I've left thee now; but though 'neath fairer skies,
Where cloud-capped mountains prop the bending heavens
And nobler streams go murmuring through the vales
And bathe the granite foot of greener hills,
Yet when the day is done, and I am sad,
And fond Remembrance from her temple brings
Her diamond treasures, that can win the soul
Away to other scenes, I'll wander back
And linger on the banks of thy pure streams,
Or climb the wood-crowned height, and fondly gaze
On Erie's bright blue waters as they roll,
And listen to the music of their voice
That shouts to me a welcome home again.

Woodrow Wilson

1856–1924

❧

28th president (1913–21)

Woodrow Wilson tried to keep the US out of World War I. When the Allied Powers achieved victory the year after America entered the war, the president promoted an ambitious peace plan. The last of his Fourteen Points called for an international body, the League of Nations, which was the forerunner of the United Nations.

Wilson was the only president to receive a PhD. He published a dozen books and wrote for leading periodicals. He was one of the most famous professors and became the president of Princeton University.

Although Wilson often came across as reserved, his poetry demonstrated his sentimental and humorous sides. In *Poetry and the American Presidency*, Paul J. Ferlazzo wrote that Wilson actively read poetry and "deeply appreciated the ability of poets to write precisely and with feeling." Ferlazzo noted that Wilson "quotes, paraphrases, and makes reference to a great number of poets throughout" his writing. Ferlazzo added that Wilson "wrote poetry that reflected his life experiences and the wit of a highly developed intellect." Through the verse he wrote and the limericks he recited, Wilson's fondness for poetry helped to humanize him.

None of Wilson's poetry was published in his lifetime. His longest poem, "A River's Course," is more than a nature poem. In *Woodrow Wilson: The Last Romantic*, Mary Stockwell determined that it was autobiographical. She explained that the "course" went from Wilson's childhood to how his "dreams had come crashing to an end when his lady fair had refused his proposal of marriage," leaving him to "go on without his childhood dreams and his beloved." This interpretation makes sense when viewed in conjunction with "A Song," which Wilson wrote within a few weeks of "A River's Course" in 1881. In "A Song," he hoped that his lost love, Hattie Woodrow, would return to him. Stockwell observed, "The shortness of this second poem, when set against the great length of 'A River's Course,' betrayed his own suspicion that this would never happen. His despair filled pages, but his hope could only fill one stanza."

By the time Wilson penned "To E. L. A. on Her Birthday" in 1884, he had fallen for another "lady fair," Ellen Louise Axson. The genethliacum, or birthday poem, praises her and expresses his love. They wed the following year.

Wilson traveled by ship from Scotland to New York in 1896. He revealed his sense of humor in a poem about A. F. Nightingale, a passenger who was undaunted despite the ship's turbulence.

The final two selections are limericks. Wilson reeled off humorous limericks during campaign speeches and at least one Cabinet meeting. He recited Anthony Euwer's "As a beauty I'm not a great star" limerick so often that many people thought Wilson had written it. The first limerick selection is well-known in limerick circles and widely attributed to Wilson. In *The Lure of the Limerick*, William S. Baring-Gould called it "a gem." In *The Pentatette*, Arthur Deex posited, "Although there does not appear to be a primary source for the Wilson/Duchess authorship (and I suspect there is none), what really matters is that everyone *thinks* that Wilson wrote it."

The second limerick comes from *The Political Education of Woodrow Wilson* by James Kerney, an adviser to Wilson who served as special ambassador to Haiti. He recalled that during a meeting two months before Wilson passed away, he delivered a limerick "of his own" with "considerable glee." According to Kerney, Wilson "had recently put together" the limerick to "amuse—or perhaps shock—a rather prim woman friend."

A River's Course

I know a deep river that chafes with its shores
And roars with rage at its bondage,
Surlily turning its quick currents about
When crossed by rocks in its voyage.

With hisses and sighs its dark currents run down
The grim, frowning mountains between,
Leaping fiercely and high o'er hindering crags,
Or skulking in gorges unseen.

When at last it has forced its rough, toilsome way
Past the outmost spurs of the chain,
It quietly steals 'long the edge of the mead,
As if courting good humor again.

Good humor returned with the sunlight and ease,
It speeds briskly over green fields,
Until, cooling itself under green-grown banks,
Into a thick forest it steals.

In the depths of the wood its waters divide,
Encircling a bleak island rock,
From whose towering height a gray castle looms,
Which is dumb to the stranger's knock.

Where a narrow bridge spans the stream to the east
A windowless tower rises,
Its sheer sides built high in embattled strength,
Its one gate barred, 'gainst surprises.

From this frontal tower stretch the winding curves
Of walls that are scarred with traces
Of fierce assaults made with hot, maddened hate
By proud princes of dead races.

Within in the wall's embrace towers marked by time
Rear high their gray, turretted crests,
Draping their sides in clinging ivy, that hides
The wan wrinkles roughing their breasts.

The inner courts and great halls of this castle
Never now hear the tread of men;
Where feasting was regal now screams the eagle
And grow the rank weeds of the fen.

The owls find homes in its vaulted roofs and domes;
The moss grows rank in its chambers;
Its windows are draped with the light silken webs
Which spiders spin 'tween their slumbers.

In dining hall rots the old oaken table;
In bed-room the garniture moulds;
The tapestries stiffen and crack as with pain
When the winds sport amongst their folds.

The alarm bell up in that crumbling turret
In silence has rusted its tongue;
The only sound that e'er rouses its temper
Is the chirp of the sparrows' young.

The winds that oft wander in wild wantonness
Through the desolate corridors
Shriek shrill with delight at the lorn loneliness,
And slam in rough sport the doors.

Where the walls creep down to the swift water's edge
And stand with their feet in the flood,
The tide hastens past the falling ruin aghast
As if fearing some stain of blood.

The streams pass the island with hurrying flow,
With a rush both frightened and fleet,
Till, beyond the forbidding and gloomy pile,
Their currents caressingly meet.

With darkened faces the wedded currents race off
Moaning, as a burden of song,
Notes that now sigh, and anon rise in a cry,
Like mem'ries of unrevenged wrong.

When the river has quit the thick forest shades
And entered a bustling city,
Men do not ween what saddest things it has seen,
What signs of death and of pity.

Running briskly past the noisy town so vast,
The river flows merrily on,
Till its waters meet and unchafingly greet
Banks of green, gently-sloping lawn.

Not with brilliant flowers and trellised bowers
Are these grassy slopes surrounded;
Great oaks stretch their shades over deep, silent glades
Where the velvety turf is bounded.

Beyond the broad stretches of the pleasant lawn
A goodly mansion stately stands,
With windows wide and many a shading porch,
The manor house of ample lands.

On the grass two merrily romping brothers
Are playing in free, childish glee:
A lovely lady they call to as "mother"
Is laughing their gladness to see.

His mistress's laugh, so joyous and cheery,
From his place in the grateful sun
Rouses the great sleeping dog from slothful dreams
And sends him to join in the fun.

Breezes make the great oaks in the groves to nod
In monotonous melody;
Gleeful birds sport and sing in the silvan courts
Many an artless rhapsody.

The river takes up in musical ripples
Echoes of the sweet lady's laugh;
It answers the songs of the leaves and the birds,
And its heart seems lighter by half.

Its journey's now short to the bed of the sea,
But its pace is none the less fleet
Till it peacefully pours its waters, at last,
Out at old Ocean's briny feet.

A Song

Sing, ye feathered songsters,
Sing in full concert all your quaintest strains,
Each richest note that melody contains,
Each pleasant chord, each harmony sonorous
Join ye in one ringing chorus;
Your voices raise in sweetest praise:
My love is won and joy fills all my days.

To E. L. A. on Her Birthday

I cannot tell, my lady fair,
What thine own thoughts may be
When that thou comest once again
Thy natal day to see;

But this I know, and fain would tell
Close at thy listening ear,
That God has given few gifts more blest
Than this thy closing year.

Bright as thy frank and laughing eyes
Should be this blest May-day,
And radiant as thy loving smile
Its sun's flower-kissing ray.

Thy sorrows past are hallowed all
By deeds of duteous love;
They speak to thee of gladness given
To that dear one above.

They testify of love's glad care
For duties thou did'st bear
To make thy home again as bright
As when her form was there.

That home was stricken, not in wrath
For sin, or shame, or wrong,
But that in God our trust might stand
And in his strength be strong.

Why should'st thou not thy birthday hail
With joy and hope and mirth?
How sad soe'er thy life has been
God smiled upon thy birth.

For thee he sent to blessings bear
Of love and sympathy,
To show to us the beauty rare
Of brave work's majesty.

He sent thee to make bright the lives
And ease the arduous part
Of those to whom thou wast to bring
Thy purity of heart.

He gave to thee in largess free
Not only beauty's charm,
But all the graces that win man
And stay him from his harm.

Thou art thyself his chiefest gift
To him to whom 'tis given
To see in thy sweet, trusting eyes
The love for which he's striven.

If that thou think'st it good to be
On such blest missions sent,
Can'st thou not smile e'en o'er the year
That's been so sadly spent?

This fair May-day sure seems to me
A rose without its thorn;
For can there be aught ill in this,
The day when thou wast born?

Until I saw thy winsome face
And love-light in thine eyes,
I had not known the fairest forms
Born 'neath these May-day skies.

But now I can believe that this,
The hey-day of the Spring,
Is fairest month in Nature's round
For that it thee did bring!

On Board Steamship Anchoria

The man who was never daunted
By summons to regale,
Nor yielded up nor fainted,
Our lusty Nightingale.

What though the good ship was pitching
And straining at every sail,
He held his own unshaken,
Our doughty Nightingale.

All praise to the stout retainer,
So self-contained and hale,
Who kept his faith with nature,
Our wholesome Nightingale.

I sat next to the Duchess at tea;
It was just as I feared it would be:
    Her rumblings abdominal
    Were truly phenomenal,
And everyone thought it was me!

There was a young girl from Missouri
Who took her case to the jury.
    She said, "Car Ninety-three
    Ran over my knee."
But the jury said, "We're from Missouri."

Warren G. Harding

1865–1923

29ᵗʰ president (1921–23)

Historians remember Warren G. Harding as an ineffectual, unpopular president. Lowlights include adulterous sexcapades, restricted immigration, and the Teapot Dome scandal, in which his secretary of the interior profited from leasing federal oil reserves.

While Harding worked as a newspaper writer and editor prior to his political career, his most enduring legacy as a man of letters is his letters.

Harding had an affair with Carrie Fulton Phillips for fifteen years, and from 1910 to 1920, he sent her 106 letters, amounting to approximately 1,000 pages. After he won the Republican nomination for president in 1920, she threatened to release the letters and demanded hush money. A historian came across Phillips's collection in 1963. Harding's family sued to keep it private for a half century. Upon its release in 2014, *The New York Times* noted, "The correspondence is intimate and frank—and perhaps the most sexually explicit ever by an American president. Even in the age of Anthony Weiner sexts and John Edwards revelations, it still has the power to astonish." In the love letters, Harding refers to his genitalia as Jerry and professes his "mad, tender, devoted, ardent, eager, passion-wild, jealous, reverent, wistful, hungry, happy love."

In addition to sending Phillips others' poems, Harding wrote eight rhyming originals for her. The first six selections were written between 1912 and 1914, and the last two are undated. He sent some as stand-alone verse and interpolated others into his prose. The romantic and erotic content ranges from the straightforward, with tedious adulation, to the metaphorical, with an elaborate maritime construction. "Adrift in Reverie: With Apologies to No One but You" presents a pornographic fantasy, with the parentheses at the ends of the stanzas guiding the narrative through escalation, climax, and postcoital reflection. Some poems are occasional, tied to the lovers' seven-year anniversary and Christmas. Harding does not shy away from the reality that he and Phillips are having an extramarital affair, considering its implications for the present and future. This anthology is the first coherent publication of Harding's verse. Some poems have redundant concepts, wording, and rhymes. Harding surely did not consider this shortcoming and how it might be perceived when the poems were juxtaposed more than a century later. According to Karen Linn Femia, an archivist who organized Harding's letters for the Library of Congress, he intended his poems for an audience of one. She opined, "It would be unfair to judge him against real poets. He was never that."

I love your face
When all aglow
I love your hair
When tresses flow.

I love your mouth
With nectar sweet
Love every inch
From head to feet.

I love your voice
I love your smiles
I love your laugh
When it beguiles.

I love your cheeks
And neck so fair
I love your arms
And shoulders bare.

I love your back
I love your breasts
Darling to feel
Where my face rests.

I love your skin
So soft and white
So dear to feel
And sweet to bite.

I love your hips
So shapely, mine!
I love perfection—
Your form divine!

I love your knees
Their dimples kiss
I love your ways
Of giving bliss.

I love your poise
Of perfect thighs
When they hold me
In paradise.

I love your fresh
And sweet perfume
Love your incense
Love to consume.

I love the rose
Your garden grows
Love sea shell pink
That over it glows.

I love the dew
Your lips distill
I love the joy—
I always will.

I love to suck
Your breath away
I love to cling—
There long to stay.

I love your warmth
I love your fire
I love the way
You stir desire.

I love your size
And daintiness
Love every thread
In which you dress.

I love you garb'd
But naked, *more!*
Love your beauty
To thus adore.

I love your hands—
Their touch, caress
I love you for
Your gentleness.

I love your hopes
Your high ideals
I love the soul
Your love reveals.

I love you most
Somehow or other
Because you're best
As a mother.

I love you for
Your noble thought;
And helpfulness
To me you brought.

I love you pure
And cold as snow;
I love you when
On fire, aglow!

I love your wish—
Your best intent.
Love your honor
By Heaven sent.

I love the light
In eyes and face
And the rapture
Of your embrace.

I love your touch
Your kindling flame
Love every thing
And love acclaim.

I love to have
You transport me
I love you to
A wanton be—

When you give all
Inspired by kiss
To send me to
The realms of bliss.

I love you when
You open eyes
And mouth and arms
And cradling thighs.

I love you all
And all the time
I want you all
You *must* be mine.

I love so much—
Where shall I stop?
There! Let me say—
Last precious drop!

How shall *we* say "good night," my dearest—
How shall we end the long day?
I would bring you to my heart nearest
And hold you all night's dark way.

The day is agone, night's now stealing,
Dropping sable curtains down.
What is the sweetest way appealing
To cure ev'ry hurt and frown?

Would you have an assurance spoken—
"I love! Admire! Do adore!"
Or shall it be an ardent token
Of heart aflame, yea, and more?

How much the day with love inspiring,
Did you rejoice or sorrow?
Can't we forget the day expiring—
Expecting more tomorrow?

We will. There's no changing days gone by,
Good or bad, with lessons learned.
Let us for morrow's victory try—
Achieving a triumph earned.

Alone, in love, secure, possessing,
There's our *universe* for two.
My heart so full, so glad, confessing
All its love, *just all for you.*

Now, how to give to wish insisting,
    Its expression *best* tonight?
The sweetest joy of love enlisting—
    Some indulgence of delights?

Shall wild be our kisses, awaking
    The glowing flame of desire—
Till hearts and bodies grow to aching
    Love's flame, a melting, on fire?

How can one kiss, moist, be suffering?
    Tasting makes mad for a feast.
I'll want full a hundred, enticing,
    Hundreds of dear ones, at least.

Perhaps such a thought makes you fear it,
    And wish to speed my caress.
Well, I'm so glad holding you dear, that
    I'll yield, even though I possess.

Like joy rising in little or all—
    To end the blessings of day—
I could wait for your heart's love to call
    Me to yours, its dearest way.

It may be you're weary in trying
    To smooth out ruffles today.
Very well, let me hold you just lying
    Cradled close, in love's own way.

I want to feel your breasts, so freighted
    In dear love and ampleness,
Close to my heart, with much love weighted
    Soothed *thus* by their tenderness.

I'll hold you close, fitting loins to hips,
   Your head on a loving arm,
Asking there that you give me your lips
   While I kiss away alarm.

Oh, yes, I'd crave my eyes' enjoyment—
   Of beauty beyond compare;
And all the joys of love's employment
   Fondling you, my wondrous fair!

True! I'd wish experience, sending
   Me to gates of paradise—
Your open lips, eyes, arms, extending,
   And the pillowing of thighs.

But if you're blue, as I am, sweetheart,
   Caring not for passion's flame,
We'll remain serene, hold *that* apart,
   Whispering *love* to speak your name.

There is *such* peace and joy, adoring,
   Clasping you so close tonight.
For *knowing* this, I'm God imploring—
   "Make your morrow, glad and bright."

For such sweet peace in this possession—
   Such heart's ease where oft forlorn—
Let this the end be of obsession,
   Wake me not when [unfinished]

Speed on, good ship, if you but bring
That which I crave, that dearest thing
　　Of all, save her alone;
Make haste and land the missive dear
For which I long—my heart to cheer—
　　My lonesomeness atone!

Breach wave! Brave storm! Steam on to bay!
Where you, in calm, at dark may lay,
　　And yield your cargo there.
If you but knew, your gallant crew
Would shorten days and make them few—
　　To loving message bear.

Your way is long and hazard-fraught,
And journey's end oft dearly fought—
　　In battling with the seas;
But you bear gold, in written words,
Sweeter by far than the song of birds—
　　They mean so much to me!

Bring me, O ship, the lines I crave,
The written love to you she gave—
　　Her love I hold so dear!
They'll soothe the heart—this far away—
That thirsts and hungers, night and day,
　　And make me feel more near.

Mayhap, she wrote her longings sweet,
And these *my* wistfulness will meet,
   And kindle fire divine!
You'd hurry, ship, with speeding keel,
If you but knew the joy I feel
   To *read that she is mine.*

Your tons of freight and human throng
All confident in craft so strong
   Do not so much concern.
I want from her the written lines
To utter love my heart so pines—
   Which constantly I yearn.

When storms delay, I "storm" the more;
When seas impede, my lot is sore—
   Impatient at delay.
Please do make up your loss of time
And bring me love from *sweetheart, mine!*
   And make me glad today.

I hope she'll write she craves a bliss
That only comes when we may kiss—
   And *all that kiss implies;*
And ask embrace, with love-lit face,
In aching arms; there find her place.
   O, Dream of Paradise!

The Seventh Anniversary

When it is said no love endures,
  But fades in seven years—
You *know* of one so wholly yours,
  Which time itself endears.

Seven years ago you heard spoken
  The love of heart and soul:
Now, today, I send you token
  Of that love, since made whole.

Halting, nervous, I then told thee
  Amid emotions whirled;
Now, I write, I love you truly
  More than all in the world.

So, more and more, and ever more,
  Love grows in *trinity*:
And I worship and crave—adore
  You, my Divinity!

I love you with my blood on fire,
  And love you, passion free;
It is sane and sure—without desire,
  And *wild* in ecstasy.

Have what you wish—it's all your own,
  To *hold* a treasure trove.
Exalted sit, here is your throne—
  This heart of mine in love.

Who cares now what was wrought today
Of the medley that fate has whirled?
I hold you in my arms to say—
I love you more than all the world.

We *loved* today, let's dream tonight
So we may thus repeat that bliss;
Then hail, *in arms*, a new day bright
With exquisite and loving kiss.

Possessed, possessing, our loves true—
Night is heaven and day is life!
So I repeat, dear, I love you!
I'll be your lover, *you my wife!*

A Christmas note to you, sweetheart,
  Tribute of love, including,
If only kisses could have their part—
  While all the world excluding
    Caress and fondling I would add
    Just to make my own heart glad.

I have the wish, the mad desire
  To overwhelm, with hearts aglow,
And set your darling breast afire
  With such flames as lovers know:
    Then give and take, enrapt with you
    Together drinking of love's brew.

Since this can't be—we must forego—
  I'll write the things I'm feeling,
Trusting mem'ry that you know,
  To help my words' appealing.
    Thus will make remembrance dear
    And, in fancy, come precious near.

I think you fit to worship, and
  Admire, adore—possessing;
Union of soul, heart, mind and hand,
  The full bestowed blessing:
    If I could choose of all gifts known
    I'd like you, dear, for all my own.

I'd like you *now*, tomorrow, too,
  With all your love impelling—
Next week, next year, to always woo,
  And all your love compelling.
    I'd have you *now* with passion rife
    And hold you dear thro' all of life.

I love you more than all the world,
  Possession *whole* imploring,
Mid passion I am ofttimes whirled,
  Ofttimes admire—adoring.
    Oh, God! If only fate would give
    Us privilege to love and *live!*

I pray for this, my wish today—
  To have, to hold, rejoicing—
Then give to love unhampered sway
  And all my fondness voicing
    Ah, me! For such sweet fate as this,
    And know the ecstasies of bliss.

I'm wild ofttimes to madly yield—
  The last sweet drop outpouring—
While you, fair goddess, scepter wield
  When I to bliss am soaring.
    Darling, charming, rapture giving—
    You're first and best of *all* living.

I have you now *so* little, sweet,
   That it is oft distressing
To contemplate we seldom meet
   When both desire *possessing.*
      But let us hope, believe and trust
      Our happiness will come. *It must!*

So then, my Christmas wish is this—
   With all my love expressing—
That you know happiness and bliss
   And ev'ry dreamt-of blessing
      All the joys that a lover brings
      And joys of love your own heart sings.

Nay, more! Content, high hope, much joy,
   Experiences fulfilling!
And pleasure ample, none to cloy,
   The *best in life*, God willing!
      Then let me come and be a part,
      And hold my place in your dear heart.

A Sufferer's Good Wish

This wild heart, all loving, calls—
Reasoning head says nay.
Revelation so appalls—
What can one's reason say?
    This love that *we thought* all mine,
      As holy as intense,
    Calls another to be thine
      For its recompense.

There is none, then, all so pure,
In body, mind and soul,
That *one couple* can endure
And hold it sacred, whole.
    Where can hope sustain belief—
      Where anger drops its stain
    And makes hunger wish relief
      In old embrace again?

Oh, well! 'Twas heavenly dream—
    Believing you all mine—
And love hopes you may e'er glean
    All happiness in time.

Adrift in Reverie: With Apologies to No One but You

Idling, sitting, dreaming, intent on reverie,
I'm thinking of my Carrie, darling-est to me!
Retrospecting richly of vespers' worship hour,
Reveling in memory, all its joys devour.
          —(a kiss here)—

Thirsty, hungry, wistful, eager to possess,
Fancy will anticipate, in craving sweet caress.
I bring my sweetheart to me, aching to know
Possession surpassing, all aflame to grow.
          —(another kiss now)—

Open, flaming grate fire, shedding mellow light
And amply giving warmth to make conditions right.
Then to have my Carrie, just in mantle blue—
Won't you come, my darling, while I worship you?
          —(a kiss, consenting)—

I'll speak of love surpassing, dearest ever told;
Bestow admiring glances—awakened to behold
Handsomest of women—no other to compare
To you with beauty freshest, fairest of the fair.
          —(a kiss of admiration)—

Little wonder, truly, that I so much adore;
Nor any wonder, either, since always loving more,
That I revere you deeply and pay tribute, too,
With a love that's constant—ever *truly I do*!
          —(a kiss to prove)—

So, in fancy calling, you my goddess be!
Grant the widest privilege, willingly, to me.
Tell me with lips, and eager eyes inspiring,
To love you with passion, never fear of tiring!
  —(a kiss and caress here)—

Since consent is granted and the moments few,
I'll begin by kissing where lips of honied dew
Intoxications offer, like no other known,
And make me wild! Let restraint away be thrown!
  —(a kiss with fondling now)—

Loving, kissing, *drinking*, let us once feel free
To let lips go a kissing from eye-lids to knee.
Stopping often, supping, on your nectar'd lips
But bent on going, *often*, on alluring trips.
  —(kiss again, with caresses)—

I know they'll stop and linger, sucking to test
The wine that's ever brimming o'er beauty of breast.
Circumspecting gladly all the darling way
Where lips are often puzzled—longest place to stay.
  —(a double kiss here)—

Sipping, feasting gladly, many joys they meet
But after all cling most on ruby lips so sweet;
Breaching your existence, making hearts to flutter,
Feeling—so delicious, words can never utter!
  —(Let a long kiss tell here)—

Melting, burning blisses, lips in kissing twine
To mingle soul and spirit, and bodies incline
To encompass each the other, in abandon's sway—
Entwined in trance of rapture, heavenly to play!
    —(Ask hands and lips and eyes)—

Not yet, tempting darling! Prelude is not done.
Fondling is not finished, tho' 'tis well begun.
Patting lips exquisite always adds to fire—
I must kiss and *bite* them, to satisfy desire.
    —(and do it right here)—

Having had experience, you know when my eyes
Must seek a garden's beauty, twixt your shapely thighs.
Let me feel and fondle—lips of sea shell pink,
And breathe perfume of heaven, on the very brink.
    —(May n't I, right now?)—

Being mine *so wholly*, I must kiss you there,
Inhaling, sensing, fragrance found no other where.
Chastest, sweetest freshness! God! How it allures!
And fascinates, intoxicates, tempts and endures!
    —(Carrie, *Darling*)—

No longer let's deny; yonder bed's inviting
Two *hungerers* to supremest of delighting.
Let me wish *you*, darling, while you're clipping me
The most and best joy ever—*mine your pleasure be!*
    —(a kiss of mutuality)—

Kissing, fondling, *drinking*, near the fire aglow,
Make me madly eager the *greater* joy to know.
Let us go then, where, in answer to my sighs,
You open lips and arms, and perfect, cradling thighs.
            —(Best in the world)—

In this weld divinest, plighting troth anew,
We'll wed, and pour *oblation*, dearest we can do.
Consecrating, crowning, you my wife to be—
I'll swear you fidelity for eternity.
            —(Can't you believe?)—

Carrie, take me, panting, to your heaving breast;
In thrilling rapture sinking, in your embrace's rest.
Sweetheart! Joy! O, God! It's thus I'd wish to die,
And awake to resurrection—in your arms to lie.
            —(Ineffable, incomparable)—

Fiercely, sweetly, grand! All my soul a filling,
And freighting ev'ry nerve, thro' my body thrilling,
You're taking me! In ecstatic pleasure rife,
And I the *last drops* give you, precious one of life!
            —(Would you?)—

Thus went vesper worship, basking 'fore the fire,
Modified or amplified, sweet as Devonshire.
In Montreal or Boston were no grates aglow—
Yet *darling-est* experience I can ever know.
            —(Mine, you're mine!)—

Ronald Wilson Reagan

1911–2004

40th president (1981–89)

Ronald Wilson Reagan's presidency was responsible for economic prosperity domestically. His "peace through strength" foreign policy agenda helped usher in the end of the Cold War.

Reagan was called the Great Communicator because of his oratorical skills, which were linked to his abilities as a writer and an actor. As a youth, Reagan adored a book of poetry by Robert W. Service. Reagan memorized and enjoyed reciting at least two of Service's poems.

At seventeen, Reagan wrote "Life" for his high school yearbook, the *Dixonian*. "Life" is more substantive than the standard fare from teenage poets. Considering life's hardships, the existential poem expresses the signature optimism that Reagan would come to be known for.

When he was the governor of California, he again wrote poetry for a publication geared toward high school students. The Scholastic magazine *Literary Cavalcade* solicited poems from prominent politicians. In his cover letter, Reagan said, "It is important that politicians show that they are capable of at least trying to write poetry. It is a challenge." In "Time," most of the content is a list poem, detailing what kept Reagan busy during his governorship. The final three lines note that even though eight years have elapsed, the tree outside his window "looks just the same." *Literary Cavalcade* declined to publish Reagan's second submission, "State Budget," because of quality concerns.

Life

I wonder what it's all about, and why
We suffer so, when little things go wrong?
We make our life a struggle,
When life should be a song.

Our troubles break and drench us,
Like spray on the cleaving prow
Of some trim Gloucester schooner.
As it dips in a graceful bow.

Our troubles break and drench us
But like that cleaving prow,
The wind will fan and dry us.
And we'll watch some other bow.

But why does sorrow drench us
When our fellow passes on?
He's just exchanged life's dreary dirge
For an eternal life of song.

What is the inborn human trait
That frowns on a life of song?
That makes us weep at the journey's end,
When the journey was oft-times wrong?

Weep when we reach the door
That opens to let us in,
And brings to us eternal peace
As it closes again on sin.

Millions have gone before us,
And millions will come behind.
So why do we curse and fight
At a fate both wise and kind.

We hang onto a jaded life
A life full of sorrow and pain.
A life that warps and breaks us,
And we try to run through it again.

Time

Budgets
Battles
Phone calls
Hassles.
Letters
Meetings
Luncheons
Speeches.
Politics and
Press Releases.
News conferences
Delegations
Plaques and
Presentations.
Travels
Briefings
Confrontations.
Crises
Routines
Meditation.
Eight years passes swiftly.
But I look out the window.
The elm in the park looks just the same.

Appendix A: Four Additional Presidents Who Wrote Poetry

The original plan for *Poems by Presidents* featured poems by several other presidents. Due to practical obstacles, their selections could not be included. Nevertheless, these presidents belong in the conversation.

Jimmy Carter

Jimmy Carter wrote over thirty books, more than any president other than Theodore Roosevelt. Although he focused on nonfiction, his works include a novel, *The Hornet's Nest*, and a fairy-tale picture book, *The Little Baby Snoogle-Fleejer*. He won the Grammy Award for Best Spoken Word Album—based on his books—thrice, more than any other president.

Carter's interest in poetry began in his youth and stuck with him. His eighth-grade English teacher required her students to memorize famous poems and write their own verse. When Carter was in the Navy in 1948–52, he spent stretches of multiple days on a submarine and penned poems to help pass the time. He composed love poems for his wife, Rosalynn, and wrote about happenings on the vessel. At Carter's inaugural gala in 1977, James Dickey read a poem. Before working on a poetry book, Carter sought guidance from Miller Williams and James Whitehead and "received the equivalent of a postgraduate course in poetry," as he put it.

In 1995, Carter published the *New York Times* bestseller *Always a Reckoning and Other Poems*. He became the first president to publish a collection of poems in his lifetime—and aside from John Quincy Adams's epic poem, it is the only poetry book published by a living president. Carter dedicated it, in part, to readers who "will draw from [the poems] some pleasure, stimulating thoughts, or memories to make up for my lack of erudition, skill, or artistry." There is a mix of free verse and rhyming poems. In addition to a haiku about Mount

Fuji, a fourteen-word quatrain about war, and a sonnet about Carter's hometown of Plains, Georgia, selections discuss peanuts, Rosalynn, a submarine, and the universe.

The book's forty-five poems are divided into four sections: People, Places, Politics, and Private Lives. Many poems explore people, locations, and circumstances from Carter's lived experiences. His modus operandi can be found in the poem "Itinerant Songsters Visit Our Village": "I learned from poetry that art/is best derived from artless things." In other words, he draws on real life.

In *Poetry and the American Presidency*, Paul J. Ferlazzo observed that Carter's "over-riding decency and generosity come through without any hint of pride or preachiness." Ferlazzo added, "There is present in the poems some country wit, some sly humor, some cleverness, and very little irony."

According to *Booklist*, *Always a Reckoning and Other Poems* is "about half lightly nostalgic, often keenly evocative, autobiographical narratives and half blunt and simple reflections of his famously charitable political and social convictions."

Carter was not aware of the scope of presidential poetry. "I have heard it said that John Quincy Adams and Abraham Lincoln wrote poems, but I have never seen any of their poems," he explained while promoting his book in a television interview. "I've asked two or three people lately who were poetry critics if they had read the poems of the two previous presidents. They said no."

To listen to Carter read "Rachel" and "The Pasture Gate" and watch him recite "Considering the Void," visit the bonus material webpage for *Poems by Presidents* at www.doverpublications.com/0486851532. Links are provided for five additional poems by Carter: "Rosalynn," "Some Things I Love," "A Reflection of Beauty in Washington," "Progress Does Not Always Come Easy," and "Itinerant Songsters Visit Our Village."

George Bush

George Bush was one of only five sitting presidents to write poetry, but his poems are not accessible.

In *The Quiet Man* (2015), his chief of staff, John H. Sununu, recalled that Bush penned limericks about world leaders while at the conference of the Commission on Security and Cooperation in Europe in 1990. Sununu wrote, "I made sure to destroy all the notes. The only lines I clearly remember, or maybe the only ones I am subconsciously willing to divulge, were one that started, 'There was a big Chancellor from Bonn . . .' and another that ended, 'Only Denis, her husband, could catch her.'" The subjects were Helmut Kohl, chancellor of Germany, and Margaret Thatcher, prime minister of the UK, respectively. However, in 2018, Sununu claimed that he still had all the limericks and added that "a couple had a bit of an R rating!"

The George H. W. Bush Presidential Library has no record of the limericks. Multiple attempts to reach Sununu were unsuccessful.

Barack Obama

When Barack Obama was a student at Occidental College, he published two poems in *Feast*, one of the school's literary magazines, in spring 1982. This was apparently the first time that the nineteen-year-old publicly identified himself as Barack, rather than Barry. When the poems resurfaced in 2007, Eric Newhall, an English professor who was a faculty advisor for *Feast*, noted they showcase that Obama "does have a way with language and with imagery."

Obama wrote "Pop" for a contemporary poetry class. In this autobiographical poem, he discusses an encounter with his maternal grandfather, Stanley Dunham, also known as Pop. From Pop's perspective, Obama is "a green young man" who does not fully take into account the "Flim and flam of the world."

"Underground" is much shorter and more experimental. The opening lines indicate that the setting is "Under water grottos, caverns/Filled with apes." Harold Bloom, an English professor at Yale University, was reminded of D. H. Lawrence's verse: "I think it is about some sense of chthonic forces, just as Lawrence frequently is—some sense, not wholly articulated, of something below, trying to break through."

At a poetry workshop and reading at the White House in 2015, Obama quipped, "'President' is a cool title, but 'former teen poet'— that is a pretty good title as well. And I'm proud to be both." He spoke about the importance of poetry:

> Poetry matters. Poetry, like all art, gives shape and texture and depth of meaning to our lives. It helps us know the world. It helps us understand ourselves. It helps us understand others—their struggles, their joys, the ways that they see the world. It helps us connect. . . . I think it's fair to say that if we didn't have poetry that this would be a pretty barren world. In fact, it's not clear that we would survive without poetry.

To read "Pop" and "Underground," visit the bonus material webpage for *Poems by Presidents* at www.doverpublications.com/0486851532.

Joseph R. Biden

Joseph R. Biden's mother and great-grandfather both wrote poetry. In his teens, Biden overcame his stutter in part because he recited poetry by William Butler Yeats in front of a mirror.

According to Biden, he has "had a lifelong love for Irish poets." When he was the vice president, he quoted Yeats's "Easter 1916" in twenty-one speeches. As president, he repeated Seamus Heaney's line about when "hope and history rhyme" at such varied events as the National Prayer Breakfast, the tenth anniversary of the dedication of the Martin Luther King Jr. Memorial, the centennial of the Tulsa Race Massacre, a reception for the Israeli Presidential Medal of

Honor, and a celebration of Nowruz, the Persian New Year. In an address to Ireland's parliament, Biden explained:

> I was always quoting Irish poetry. . . . And my [Senate] colleagues always thought I did it because I was Irish. That's not the reason. You're the best poets in the world. That's the reason I did it.

In 2018, Biden gave his wife, Jill, a book of original poems as a Christmas present. Her favorite includes this couplet: "I worked so hard to get you to say I do/When you did—you made the world anew." During a television interview in 2022, she revealed that he adds a new poem to the book by hand for Christmas each year. "I have a lot to write about," replied the president as he grabbed her hand.

Appendix B: Misattributions

Some readers might have expected three other presidents to make the cut. The poems associated with the following presidents were misattributed.

Herbert Clark Hoover

Herbert Clark Hoover widely read poetry, and he appreciated its potential. He said, "Perhaps what this country needs is a great poem. Something to lift people out of fear and selfishness. . . . Sometimes a great poem can do more than legislation." Despite the impressions of many Australians, Hoover did not write any poetry.

Hoover worked as a mining engineer in Western Australia in the late 1890s. In 1933, the last year of his presidency, Australian journalist Arthur Reid published what he called Hoover's "erotic and exotic verses" in *Those Were the Days*. Reid alleged that Hoover wrote the poem to a former barmaid in the area of the goldfields, years after he had departed:

Do you ever dream my sweetheart, of a twilight long ago,
Of a park in old Kalgoorlie, where the bouganvileas grow,
Where the moonbeams on the pathways trace a shimmering
    brocade
And the overhanging peppers form a lovers' promenade.
Where in soft cascades of cadence from a garden close at hand,
Came the murmurous mellow music of a sweet orchestral band,

Years have flown since then, my sweetheart, fleet as orchard
    blooms in May;
But the hour that fills my dreaming, was it only yesterday?

Stood we two a space in silence, while the summer sun slipped
  down,
And the grey dove dusk with drooping pinions wrapt the mining
  town,
Then you raised your tender glances darkly, dreamily to
  mine,
And my pulses clashed like symbols in a rhapsody divine.
And the pent-up fires of longing loosed their prison's weak
  control,
And in wild hot words came rushing madly from my burning soul.

Wild hot words that spoke of passion, hitherto but half expressed,
And I clasped you close my sweetheart, kissed you, strained you to
  my breast,
While the starlight spangled heavens rolled round us where we
  stood,
And a tide of bliss swept surging through the currents of our
  blood.
And I spent my soul in kisses, crushed upon your scarlet mouth.
Oh! my red-lipped sunbrowned sweetheart, dark-eyed daughter
  of the south.
It was well that fate should part us, it was well my path should
  lead,
Back to slopes of high endeavour aye, and was it well indeed.
You have wed some southern squatter, learned long since his every
  whim
Soothed his sorrows, borne his troubles, sung your sweetest songs
  for him.
I have fought my fight and triumphed, on the map I've writ my
  name,
But I prize one hour of loving, more than fifty years of
  fame.

It was but a summer madness, that possessed me, men will hold,
And the yellow moon bewitched me, with its wizardry of gold,
As they will, but ofttimes in the dusk, I close my eyes,
And in dreams drift back where stars rain silver splendour from
    the skies,
To a park in far Kalgoorlie, where the golden wattles grow,
Where you kissed me in the twilight, of a summer long ago.
And I clasp you close, my sweetheart, while each throbbing pulse
    is thrilled
By a low and mournful music that shall never more be stilled.

Australian folklore has subsequently held that Hoover wrote
the poem. At the Palace Hotel in Kalgoorlie, Australia, the poem is
displayed alongside a mirror that Hoover gifted to the hotel following
his extensive stays. "Herbert Hoover's Love Song" was set to music
and included in a book of Australian ballads, and it is still performed
in Australia.

Reid's attribution comes across as sloppy journalism, whether
deliberate or not. The first red flag is that he referred to "H. P.
Hoover," even though Hoover's middle name is Clark. In *The Life
of Herbert Hoover*, George N. Nash raised other concerns. Nash
wrote that an original copy of the poem had never been found and
questioned how Reid obtained it. Nash noted that the poem does
not match any of Hoover's other writing stylistically. Nash explained
that it was improbable that "this prominent American, now married
and in the public eye, would have written such a poem to an old
flame whom he had not seen for years," as its release would have
been "acutely embarrassing." To play devil's advocate, though, Nash
was unaware of the erotic poems written by Warren G. Harding
in roughly the same time period, and Harding's poetry shatters
conventional wisdom.

Franklin Delano Roosevelt

In *FDR's Fireside Chats*, Russell D. Buhite and David W. Levy commended Franklin Delano Roosevelt's "unique ability to communicate to the American people." Buhite and Levy said, "Roosevelt had a gift for effective language, for anecdote and metaphor and witticism. He seemed to recognize this gift and genuinely to enjoy addressing the public in one way or another." While historians focus on Roosevelt's radio addresses and inaugural speeches, the same description applies to verse associated with him, even if he did not write it.

In 1932, about a week after announcing his candidacy for president, Roosevelt, then the governor of New York, had a party for his fiftieth birthday. He recited humorous rhyming verse about attendees. His mother (referred to as Mrs. James Roosevelt), wife (Ellie Roosevelt), son (James Roosevelt), daughter (Anna), daughters-in-law (Betty and Betsey), and son-in-law (Curtis Dall) were among the family at the celebration. Other guests included Roosevelt's lieutenant governor (Governor Lehman), future secretary of the Treasury (Henry Morgenthau), and law partners (Langdon Marvin and Harry Hooker).

Roosevelt repeatedly used the first person in the poems, and some writers have attributed authorship of various excerpts to the man who uttered them. On a transcript of the verse provided by the Franklin D. Roosevelt Presidential Library, handwritten notes include "by whom?" and "F. D. R. says *not* by him, tho' he may have 'had a hand' in some of the verses."

Another guest, Sam Rosenman, has shed light on how the writing process might have worked. Rosenman was already a speechwriter for Roosevelt, and he became the head of speechwriting at the White House. In *Working with Roosevelt*, Rosenman explained that speeches Roosevelt gave as president were "his—and his alone." According to Rosenman, "They all expressed the personality, the convictions, the spirit, the mood of Roosevelt. No matter who worked with him in the preparation, the finished product was always the same—it was Roosevelt himself." While Roosevelt might not have written all of the verse, he likely helped shape the manuscript so that he would be comfortable reciting it as his own words:

> **Betty**
> Why so silent, Betty dear?
> Scarce a word from you I hear.
> Is it really force of habit
> Keeps you noiseless as a rabbit?
> When alone does Elliott do
> All the talking for the two?

> **Betsey**
> Did my Eleanor relate
> All the sad and awful fate
> Of the miserable lives
> Lived by politicians' wives?
> Should Jim run for office, dear,
> Take him firmly by the ear,
> Lead him miles and miles away
> From the polls, and make him stay.

> **Marion**
> Marion once for office ran.
> Better than the rest she can
> Understand it is not wise
> Always to particularize—
> And a somewhat abstract view
> Keeps an issue safe for you.

Molly
From New Zealand came our Molly,
Which she says is very jolly.
Well, this much we can declare:
They have first-class earthquakes there.

Mrs. O'Connor
Greatly I admire and honor
She who married Doc O'Connor.
Oh, what courage, oh, what pluck,
Oh, what trusting to her luck.
From the fund of Carnegie
Medals five should come to thee.

Mrs. Rosenman
Don't let wily Samuel fool
You with tales of "better school."
Surely another reason
Makes him keep you all this season.
In Manhattan, far away,
Come up *unannounced* some day.

Mrs. James Roosevelt
Delegates from many states
Favor local candidates
But there always will be one
Place where I'm the favorite son.

Anna
Thoughtless child, what made you pray
Give your father's age away?
How can I still youthful be?
You a grandpa made of me.

Nan
In the Val-Kill shop they say
Nan has hidden safe away
(So the little birds declare)
One large presidential chair.

Ellie Roosevelt
Ellie, "racquets" used to mean
(When you were the tennis queen)
Something used to hit a ball.
Now it don't mean that at all.
Only highballs go, they say,
With the rackets of today.

Harry Hooker
[text missing]

Edmund Rogers
Those who have the strange obsession,
This is mankind's worst depression,
Are mistaken—for we know
How we felt so long ago.
When they caught us both—alas!
Breaking all the cold-frame glass.

Admiral Peoples
Man the gangway, boat ahoy.
Side boys out for Christian joy.
Welcome, Admiral, come aboard.
Take the best we can afford.

Governor Lehman

When governors are away,
Do lieutenant governors play?
Herbert Lehman tells me "no."
Well, perhaps that may be so.

Langdon Marvin

When Langdon Marvin goes to court
To argue out a case in tort
Of cunning plea or verbal fence
Of witness and of evidence,
The jury neither needs nor knows.
They're too enraptured by his clothes.

Sam Rosenman

Who turns the pardon cases down
And views parole with angry frown?
Who knows himself to be an oracle
On eloquence and things rhetorical?
Who can write messages that flow
Like Homer or like Cicero?
Who can do this and knows he can?
Why—modest Sammie Rosenman.

Henry Morgenthau

When Henry walks amid the fields,
Each turnip adoration yields.
And when he wanders past the trees,
They clap applause with all their leaves.
His agricultural skill and care
Prevent our fields from being bare.
'Tis proper that all vegetation
Should praise the boss of conservation.

James Roosevelt
He sho is filled with high ambition.
To snare the wary politician
Must softly tread, take greatest pains,
And butter freely use—oh! James.

Curtis Dall
I hear they never say "the floor"
Of stock exchanges anymore.
But, next the hard pan and the dirt
They call "cellars" Master Curt.

Louis Howe
Who writes out yards and yards of hooey
That's never used? 'Tis Little Louis.

George Radcliffe
The Heir of Redclyffe is a book
At which we now no longer look.
And lost to sight will also be
The hair of Radcliffe, too, I see.

Doc O'Connor
Who never fails to find a flaw
In any inconvenient law
And gives the judge an awful shock
By weird constructions? Sure, it's Doc.

Mrs. Marvin
It was Mrs. Marvin's pride:
Horses meddlesome to ride.
Ride them fast, and ride them furious.
And, you know, we're somewhat curious:
Won't you candidly relate
How Lang made you so sedate?

Sergeant Miller
Sergeant Miller loves to stride
Strong and stalwart by my side.
But when pretty girls go by
And attract the sergeant's eye,
What does Sergeant Miller do?
Why, he skips a step or two.

Tom Lynch
Doubling the income tax's a cinch,
But try to pay it—Thomas Lynch.

George W. Bush

As part of the National Book Festival in 2003, First Lady Laura Bush shared a poem that she said was composed by George W. Bush. She explained, "President Bush is a great leader and husband—but I bet you didn't know he is also quite the poet." The First Lady said that she had found the poem upon returning from a trip abroad, during which French President Jacques Chirac kissed her hand. She also referenced her husband's infamous speech on an aircraft carrier, in which he prematurely declared "Mission Accomplished" for major combat operations in Iraq. She clearly intended the poem as a joke, as suggested by the opening couplet, a humorous template used in children's rhymes. When the First Lady recited the poem, the audience erupted in laughter. Her husband looked uncomfortable, as though he did not appreciate being portrayed as a simplistic poet. Here is a transcription:

Dear Laura,

Roses are red;
Violets are blue.
Oh, my lump in the bed,
I've missed you.

Roses are red;
Bluer am I
Seeing you kissed
By that charming French guy.

The dogs and the cat,
They miss you too.
Barney's still mad you dropped him;
He ate your shoe.

The distance, my dear,
Has been such a barrier.
Next time you want an adventure,
Just land on a carrier.

The First Lady later insisted that her husband had not actually
written the poem. The author has never been revealed.

Appendix C: Prose Formatted as Verse

While the likes of the Watergate transcripts and social media posts from the tweeter in chief originated as prose, some people have formatted them as verse.

Calvin Coolidge

In *Author in Chief*, Craig Fehrman chronicled how Calvin Coolidge was a top-notch writer who rose to power on the success of his book *Have Faith in Massachusetts* and penned a groundbreaking autobiography. The former was a collection of Coolidge's speeches, and Fehrman described the hallmarks of Coolidge's "simple style" as "short sentences, elementary structures, and a gift for aphorism."

During a speech in Vermont in 1928, the president extolled the state where he grew up:

Vermont is a State that I love. I could not look upon the peaks of Ascutney, Whittier, and Mansfield without being moved in a way that no other scene could move me. It was here that I first saw the light of day; here that I received my bride. Here my dead lie buried, pillowed among the everlasting hills. I love Vermont because of her hills and valleys, her scenery and invigorating climate, but most of all I love her because of her indomitable people. They are a race of pioneers who almost impoverished themselves for love of others.

If ever the spirit of liberty should vanish from the rest of the Union, it could all be restored by the generous store held by the people of this brave little State of Vermont.

Several sources classified this excerpt from the speech as a poem—or prose poem—by Coolidge. In *A Rhetorical Study of the*

Speaking of Calvin Coolidge, Arthur F. Fleser presented it with poetic line breaks and praised its rhythm. He conceded, "Coolidge may not have intended this as poetry."

Some presidents, such as Abraham Lincoln and Barack Obama, incorporated poetic flourishes into their speaking and writing. Coolidge's so-called poem is in that vein. Its original context is a speech in prose.

Humor Books

A niche in humor books presents the words of various presidents as verse, although they were not written as such. These are examples of found poems, where the content is "found" in unexpected sources. Some are quite amusing when removed from their intended contexts and tweaked with line breaks, stanza breaks, and indentations.

The earliest instance is *The Poetry of Richard Milhous Nixon* (1974). Every page includes a disclaimer: "The material in this collection comes entirely from *The Watergate Transcripts*. No words or punctuation have been added, omitted, or changed in any way." The biggest source of laughter can be found in Nixon's biography on the back cover: "This is his first book of poetry."

Poetry Under Oath: From the Testimony of William Jefferson Clinton and Monica S. Lewinsky (1998) takes words verbatim from Clinton's testimony in *Paula Jones v. William Clinton* as well as from his and his mistress's testimony before a grand jury. The back cover notes that the "found poetry" is "arranged like free verse on the page."

The Anthology of Really Important Modern Poetry (2012) pokes fun at the actual statements of numerous celebrities, including the current president, Obama, and future presidents Donald J. Trump and Joseph R. Biden. Trump leads the way with six selections. The authors refer to Obama's "creative masterpiece" as a "reverse haiku" with a "7-5-7 syllabic arrangement." The introduction notes, "The time has come to celebrate the accidental lyricism of some rather unexpected wordsmiths," including "poet-vice-president foot-in-mouth-prone Joe Biden."

At least seven books twist Trump's statements from tweets and other sources into faux poems. In *The Beautiful Poetry of Donald Trump* (2017), the editor facetiously presents Trump as "an aesthete for whom love and beauty are wells of feeling to return to and draw from." The editor notes, "Whether discoursing on politics, walls, gender issues, or his own excellent genes, Trump's poems are nothing if not beautiful." Comparable titles include *The Bard of the Deal* (2015), *Make Poetry Great Again* (2016), *Donald Trump Is Unfit to Be President* (2016), *The Poetry of Donald Trump* (2018), *Collected Poetry of Donald J. Trump* (2019), and *Presidential Poetry & Inspirational Quotes* (2020).

Corn Pop: The Poetry of Joe Biden (2020) features "ramblings" pulled from Biden's speeches. The back cover explains, "Only line breaks were added to turn his words into free verse poetry."

Appendix D: Fondness for Poetry

Presidents' fondness for poetry has been a crucial part of the context for numerous presidents in this anthology. Eight additional presidents deserve mention.

John Adams carried around a book of English poetry and enjoyed reading it while on the road. When his son John Quincy Adams was a child, the elder Adams told him, "You will never be alone with a poet in your pocket." The younger Adams was the leading poet among presidents.

George Moses Horton was the only African American slave with a significant income as a poet. He transitioned from vending produce to being a public speaker and selling his poems on the campus of the University of North Carolina at Chapel Hill. Legend has it that James Knox Polk, who graduated from the school in 1818, was the first pupil to encourage him.

Theodore Roosevelt enjoyed reading a vast array of poetry. During his presidency, he championed the poetry of Edwin Arlington Robinson. Roosevelt secured a job for Robinson, pushed Scribner's to publish a new edition of his book, and wrote a book review. "It is hard to account for the failure to produce in America of recent years a poet who in the world of letters will rank as high as certain American sculptors and painters rank in the world of art," lamented Roosevelt in the review.

Harry S. Truman encountered "Locksley Hall" by Alfred, Lord Tennyson, as a teenager. He transcribed a portion of the poem on paper and always kept it in his wallet. He rewrote it twenty to thirty times through the years. Truman recounted that "Locksley Hall" had made "a very strong impression" on him because "it predicted a great many things that happened during my lifetime."

Good Housekeeping published *Dwight D. Eisenhower's Favorite Poetry, Prose and Prayers* in 1957, the year Eisenhower began his second term. This thin book features more than sixty poems that are allegedly his favorites. Samuel Taylor Coleridge, Henry Wadsworth Longfellow, William Shakespeare, and Alfred, Lord Tennyson, each have multiple selections.

John Fitzgerald Kennedy celebrated Robert Frost's poetry, including by paraphrasing one of his poems during campaign speeches. In a tradition followed by Bill Clinton, Barack Obama, and Joseph R. Biden, Kennedy was the first president to feature a poet at an inauguration, signaling the incoming administration's embrace of creatives and intellectuals. At Kennedy's inauguration, Frost recited the patriotic "The Gift Outright" as well as an excerpt from a poem he had written for the occasion, "Dedication." Kennedy later gave Frost a Congressional Gold Medal "in recognition of his poetry which has enriched the culture of the United States and the philosophy of the world." At the groundbreaking for a library posthumously named after Frost at Amherst College, Kennedy said:

When power leads men towards arrogance, poetry reminds him of his limitations. When power narrows the areas of man's concern, poetry reminds him of the richness and diversity of his existence. When power corrupts, poetry cleanses. For art establishes the basic human truth which must serve as the touchstone of our judgment.

When poet Carl Sandburg died in 1967, Lyndon Baines Johnson called him "more than the voice of America, more than the poet of its strength and genius. He was America." At a memorial service, the president eulogized, "I have no pretensions as a literary critic, but I think Carl Sandburg belongs in a very special category among poets, along with Walt Whitman."

When Gerald R. Ford was a child, his mother made him memorize Rudyard Kipling's "If." The poem begins, "If you can keep your head when. . . ." She had him recite the poem when anger took hold of him so that he would calm down.

The top resource exploring presidents' relationships with poetry is Paul J. Ferlazzo's *Poetry and the American Presidency*. Readers should consult that book for more information about Roosevelt, Truman, Kennedy, and Ford as well as other presidents mentioned earlier in this anthology.

Selected Bibliography

This bibliography is not a complete record of all works and sources. Readers who are interested in the most significant literature about poems by presidents and related topics should read the following.

Adams, John Quincy. *Dermot Mac Morrogh, or The Conquest of Ireland: An Historical Tale of the Twelfth Century: In Four Cantos.* 3rd ed. Columbus: Isaac N. Whiting, 1834.

Adams, John Quincy. *Poems of Religion and Society.* New York: William H. Graham, 1848.

Armenti, Peter. "Presidents as Poets: Poetry Written by United States Presidents." Library of Congress. Accessed January 31, 2023. https://www.loc.gov/rr/program/bib/prespoetry/index.html.

Carter, Jimmy. *Always a Reckoning and Other Poems.* New York: Times Books, 1995.

Costanzo, Michael B. *Author in Chief: The Presidents as Writers from Washington to Trump.* Jefferson, NC: McFarland & Company, Inc., Publishers, 2019.

Eisenhower, Dwight D. *Good Housekeeping Presents Dwight D. Eisenhower's Favorite Poetry, Prose and Prayers.* New York: Hearst Corp., 1957.

Fehrman, Craig. *Author in Chief: The Untold Story of Our Presidents and the Books They Wrote.* New York: Avid Reader Press, 2020.

Fehrman, Craig, ed. *The Best Presidential Writing: From 1789 to the Present.* New York: Avid Reader Press, 2020.

Ferlazzo, Paul J. *Poetry and the American Presidency.* New York: Peter Lang, 2012.

Gross, Jonathan, ed. *Thomas Jefferson's Scrapbooks: Poems of Nation, Family & Romantic Love Collected by America's Third President.* Hanover, NH: Steerforth Press, 2006.

Hirsch, Edward. *A Poet's Glossary.* Boston: Houghton Mifflin Harcourt, 2014.

Kaplan, Fred. *His Masterly Pen: A Biography of Jefferson the Writer.* New York: Harper, 2022.

Kaplan, Fred. *John Quincy Adams: American Visionary.* New York: Harper, 2014.

Kaplan, Fred. *Lincoln: The Biography of a Writer.* New York: Harper, 2008.

Lincoln, Abraham. *The Collected Poetry of Abraham Lincoln.* Springfield, IL: Lincoln & Herndon Building and Press, 1971.

Lincoln, Abraham. *The Poems of Abraham Lincoln.* Bedford, MA: Applewood Books, 1991.

Margolis, Jack S., comp. *The Poetry of Richard Milhous Nixon.* Los Angeles: Cliff House Books, 1974.

Margolis, Jeffrey A. *The President's Pen: Reflections on Presidential Literature.* Naples, FL: Great Day Bks LLC, 2020.

Petras, Kathryn, and Ross Petras. *The Anthology of Really Important Modern Poetry: Timeless Poems by Snooki, John Boehner, Kanye West and Other Well-Versed Celebrities.* New York: Workman Publishing, 2012.

Seager, Robert, II. *And Tyler Too: A Biography of John & Julia Gardiner Tyler.* New York: McGraw-Hill Book Company, Inc., 1963.

Sears, Rob, ed. *The Beautiful Poetry of Donald Trump.* Edinburgh: Canongate, 2017.

Simon, Tom, ed. *Poetry Under Oath: From the Testimony of William Jefferson Clinton and Monica S. Lewinsky.* New York: Workman Publishing, 1998.

Stockwell, Mary. *Woodrow Wilson: The Last Romantic.* New York: Nova Science Publishers, 2008.

Woodall, Guy R. "John Quincy Adams." In *Encyclopedia of American Poetry: The Nineteenth Century,* edited by Eric L. Haralson. Chicago: Fitzroy Dearborn Publishers, 1998.